Conservative,
AMERICAN AND
JEWISH

I wouldn't have it any other way.

Conservative,
AMERICAN AND
JEWISH

I wouldn't have it any other way.

By: Jacob Neusner

HUNTINGTON HOUSE PUBLISHERS

Copyright © 1993
All rights reserved. No part of this book may be reproduced without permission from the publishers, except by a reviewer who may quote brief passages in a review; nor may any part of this book be reproduced, sorted in a retrieval system, or copied by mechanical, photocopying, recording, or other means, without permission from the publisher.

Huntington House Publishers
P.O. Box 53788
Lafayette, Louisiana 70505

Library of Congress Card Catalog Number
93-78463
ISBN 1-53684-048-0

Impreso por: Editorial Presencia Ltda.
Impreso en Colombia. - Printed in Colombia.

Contents

Preface ix

Prologue A Christian Nation? We Could Do Worse xxv

PART I: What Is at Stake in Cultural Politics

Chapter 1 The West and the World: Debating the Curriculum 31

Chapter 2 Can Humanity Forget What It Knows? 35

PART II: America's Future: The Academic Battlefield

Chapter 3 What Went Wrong on the Campus 47

Chapter 4 "The Malpractice in Education Act" and Other Suggestions for Reform 57

Chapter 5 The Social Contract in the College Classroom 65

PART III: Behind the Lines: The Academic Circus

Chapter 6 The Myth of the Elite National University 75

Chapter 7 Snobs Like That Can't Happen Here 83

Chapter 8 The Coming Crisis in Ethnic Studies 87

| Chapter 9 | The Bankruptcy of Academic History | 99 |
| Chapter 10 | The Emperor's Nudist Colony | 107 |

PART IV: The Arts Endowment and the Arts

Chapter 11	It's Broke, So Fix It: Some Modest Proposals for Saving the National Endowment for the Arts	115
Chapter 12	An Endowment for the Arts, but Not This One	123
Chapter 13	Remembering the Artists: The Curse of Grace	131

PART V: The Religious Foundations of America's Social Order

Chapter 14	Talking Peace, Making War: The Paradoxical Record of Religion	137
Chapter 15	Can Someone Be "Religious in General"?	149
Chapter 16	Tolerance or Complementarity? How Religions Can Get Along in a Pluralist America	157

PART VI: The Ethnic and the Religious The Case of the Jews

| Chapter 17 | Are Jews Religious? Explaining the Religiosity of an Ethnic Group | 173 |
| Chapter 18 | Why are Jewish Neo-Cons Atheists? | 189 |

Chapter 19	Should Jews Celebrate Bastille Day?	**195**
Chapter 20	Is America the Promised Land for Jews?	**201**
Chapter 21	The Jews as the Generic Minority Group	**209**
Chapter 22	Self-Segregation in an Open Society?	**223**
Chapter 23	A Concluding Affirmation: Jews, Judaism, and Abortion	**227**

Preface

Everybody, left and right, knows that this country finds itself in the middle of a protracted civil war over culture. Begun in the aftermath of Lyndon Johnson's Great Society at home and Viet Nam excursion overseas, America's silent struggle rages—a battle for the nation's soul. The battlefields range from coast to coast, on university campuses and in their class rooms, in the arts, in the place of religion in the social order, and even in physicians' offices. Issues are political: who does what to whom; but also cultural: who teaches what to whom.

Two visions collide and, though intangible, in their collision create enormous heat, power, and above all, energy to destroy. At stake in the protracted struggle is the nation's soul: the attitudes, aspirations, and intentions that take shape long before public policy takes note but then define the character of the country. The political process merely ratifies the inner convictions that, wordlessly, take shape and coalesce in massive consensus. But we are far from any consensus. The drums still beat.

I have been a foot soldier in the struggle. In higher learning and education, the arts, and the world of religion in general and the community of Judaism in particular, I have served in the trenches. Once in a while, in odd and unanticipated circumstances, I have found myself a corporal; "After me, over the top!" This book comprises letters from the trenches, perspectives put into words in the heat of battle, sometimes on one issue, sometimes another. Here, I set forth not merely echoes of war but words spoken in the skirmishes in which, with many others, I have fought. These words are meant to make a difference—to be read beyond the day that called them forth—not because they come from a remembered past, but alas, because the issues remain urgent and moot; the armies still contend; nothing has been resolved. Nor will matters sort themselves out very soon, since subject to contention are the critical issues of the social order. I speak out of a near yesterday to a distant tomorrow.

Why should these matter? It is because all who care about our country's tomorrow—and, having passed the age of sixty, I find it natural to think a great deal about the future, as old men do—bear a heavy stake in the outcome of the war over America's culture (in German they call it *Kulturkampf*). Now, some may wonder why the character of our music and art matters in public policy, or how society has a stake in what happens in the country's colleges and universities, or whether official attitudes toward religion bear consequence for tomorrow's political decisions. Perhaps I overstate the weight of affairs. I think not.

Culture—in these pages meaning education, the arts, and religion, and, in concrete terms, universities, the National Endowment for the Arts, and the institutions of religion in general and of Judaism in particular—bears society's messages. Culture persuades, entices, and above all, dictates self-evidence, and defines and dismisses the unthinkable. The signals in words and symbols concern matters of ultimate worth that culture conveys to shape how we see things. They therefore determine how we decide matters long before politics imparts to them the concrete reality of public policy and priority. Ideas and attitudes dictate the shape of the future. Politics and public policy only ratify and give form to what people have already decided in mind and heart and soul: learning and education, the arts, and religion.

How people suppose things are, how they value

one thing and disregard another, how they imagine human beings to be—these artifacts of imagination respond to ideas and learning, take form in music and the arts, and reach expression in our prayers long before politics intervenes to attach power and even coercion to what are, to begin with, matters of hope, impalpables of heart, intellect, and soul. Society begins in imagination, in how we think things are and ought to be; only then do we go out and realize our fantasy in ordinary affairs. That is why this second civil war takes place in learning and the works of imagination, literature, art, drama, and in human aspiration, and in religion.

That explains why, in my lifetime, higher education, the arts, and religion and its place in the social order define the battlefields of the future. The sides are evenly drawn, the stakes high, and the outcome in doubt. Will universities educate, handing on a heritage of learning never intact, but forever unimpaired? Or will they serve as unelected arbiters of the social order, answerable to none in determining by criteria of social preferment—not solid achievement—what group will rise and which one will give way? Along the way, are we going to lose our heritage of learning in the transformation of the academy into a social welfare agency assigned the task of righting what are perceived as historic and continuing wrongs? Or will the academy carry forward its received assignment, to nurture intellect and to serve, and even preserve, learning out of a long, continuous past?

Control of music and the arts will determine standards of beauty and propriety. Will the arts enhance life, or degrade the soul and body? Will they lend dignity and grace to the human condition, showing us new and surprising ways to see ourselves after God's image, in God's likeness? Or will the arts despise our humanity and disgrace our vocation?

And the broadly shared conviction of Americans

that they form a people "under God," their commitment to raising children in families, their insistence that a standard of moral rectitude and responsibility for what we do govern—these established measures of the health of our social order now find themselves besieged. Militant secularism aims to exclude from legitimate discourse all religious issues and to deny God through silence; what "we all are supposed to take for granted" excludes the presence of God in the world. Zealots for the dissolution of all rules of propriety deem shame a shameful virtue; propaganda that anything is acceptable replaces those values of right and wrong that yet sustain this country's social order.

To elaborate on these simple observations concerning obvious things would answer no urgent question. Nothing of what I have said has not been articulated with greater eloquence and more effective force by the generals of the army in which I have meant to serve. The scouts, the main force, the back-ups—these have comprised remarkable, *perspicacious* figures. For the cultural war here at home, precipitated in challenges to the social order that, from the very start, addressed the university and spread beyond to culture at large, has formed the counterpart to the Cold War. But, while we have won the Cold War, we stand some distance from victory in the culture war. From the 1970s onward, in politics, the academy, and religion, great figures have taken the lead. But some of us who have served only in the trenches—the college class room, the op-ed pages of newspapers, on committees, boards, and commissions of governance of scholarship, the arts, and religious life—also have learned lessons worth sharing. That is what I wish to do by presenting a few of the essays I have written in the long struggle. It may be that others will find in them ideas they find useful, sensibility they find noteworthy, arguments they deem persuasive, and above all, a passion they hold exemplary.

So let me rapidly explain who I am and why I want to share with you a corporal's memories of the culture wars. I have gone against the stream, taking a middle-of-the-road position against extremes. The middle of the road is never crowded, but, in my case, I seem always to have walked in the wrong direction. For I am a Jewish professor in the humanities—religious studies, as a matter of fact. It ought to follow that I am a left-wing Democrat, or at least a neo-con. But that does not follow. Although I am a humanities professor and Jewish, I am by nature conservative, and by politics, conservative and Republican. I started writing for the *National Review* in the 1960s; in the seventies, my then-sister-in-law called me "Archie Bunker." She meant it as an insult, but I took it as a compliment. My career and my extra-curricular commitments as well have marked me as a person of the Right as defined by the Left, though I have always seen myself in the vital center. Sometimes the costs have mounted up, but the rewards, in the satisfaction of doing the right thing and standing for the right cause, have outweighed any momentary disappointment.

Long before grade inflation and the end of required courses (except for those required for race-, sex-, and political indoctrination), I laid my career on the line in the cause of standards of excellence in the university, the class room, and study alike. On the campus, I led the contrast when an Ivy League university dismantled its own standards of scholarly excellence in research and teaching and abandoned all pretense at education for a purpose. As a member of the National Council on the Arts, by appointment of President Reagan in 1984, I gave voice to the views of the conservative minority. I even introduced a motion at the council that federal funds not be used for partisan political purposes in the arts, and the *New Republic* paid me the compliment of an editorial titled "Jacob, the Unwise." (As is his way, the publisher then wrote me and apologized, saying he'd not seen the piece before it was printed; public offense and private apology exacts no costs on the Left.) In the Jewish community, I have taken a position against the militant secularism in command of community institutions, and, in the Judaic religion, I have maintained that a good life in Judaism is to be lived not only in the state of Israel, but also in the USA. All of these represent moderate, historically grounded positions. None of them failed to ignite its fire-storm at one time or another.

For however commonsensical, none of these positions in education, the arts, and religious life has enjoyed massive popularity, but all of them have found their vindication over time. What holds them all together and makes them form a single message relevant to a world beyond their writer is a simple, coherent proposition: we are what we do, we bear responsibility for what we are, and the future will hold us to account if we take the easy and ephemerally popular way. Mine has been a conservative position because of its moderation and simple sense.

To tell the truth, I was a conservative before I knew it, stayed a Democrat long after voting for Republicans (but made the move in 1968 anyhow and still regret not voting for Goldwater in 1964). When I was a Henry Fellow at Oxford University in 1953-1954, thirty-five years ago, I discovered that I was a conservative—not a liberal, and certainly not a Socialist. As a Jew, the discovery surprised me. I had always taken for granted that when Moses came down from Sinai, he proclaimed, "Thou shalt vote for Franklin D. Roosevelt." The Reform Temple where I grew up could have passed for the local Reform Democrat club of West Hartford, Connecticut. The prophets seemed always to be preaching the message of last year's Democratic platform, and, of, course to us, Republicans were anti-Semites, exclusivists, isolationists, practically fascists (this was in the 1940s). Democrats (the more liberal the better) stood for the good, the true, and the beautiful. So, I was a Democrat, and that meant, of course, a passionate American nationalist, who cried when he sang the "Star Spangled Banner."

In 1953 Oxford changed all that. To me, to be a Democrat meant to favor what was good for America, to be liberal in general. What I found at Oxford was that the British Left, in the early fifties, was anti-American, the Right was pro-American, and I was an American, therefore a man of the Right. We were just then emerging from the Korean War, which I firmly believed had saved South Korea from Communist aggression. But the Left in Oxford told me that we were the aggressors and should pay reparations to North Korea. These same folk—Communist dupes and fellow-travellers, as a matter of fact—had just come back from an international youth festival in Bucharest and brought with them other wonders and marvels to behold.

So shortly after arrival in September 1953, I located the Oxford University Blue Ribbon Society, the elite (so they told me) of the conservatives; for their magazine I wrote "Youth Festival in Bucharest: A Study in Fatuity." For my efforts I got roundly abused by the Socialists and happily joined the fray. I defended not what was then called McCarthyism, but the view that Communist espionage presented a serious problem to Western security. I pointed to the Soviet domination of eastern Europe and the threat to Germany. In these and other ways, I found a comfortable position in the conservative side of Oxford politics in that interesting year. When I came home, it was, of course, as a Democrat—but now as a conservative one. To my surprise, I began voting for Republicans; by the mid-1970s, the identification with the Republican party was complete. I began reading, then writing for, the *National Review* long before opponents to the American effort to save Viet Nam from Communist imperialism got rough, and I identified with the politics outlined by William F. Buckley, Jr. This was long, long before Norman Podhoretz had broken ranks. I was never a neo-con.

None of this need command your attention; it is a private story, of no compelling public interest. I am hardly unique in the personal story that I tell, except for the details. But in three chapters of my life, I found myself no longer on the sidelines, but in the center of battles. I never went in search of war, but I also never fled the fray. And I gave as good as I got. Having enemies never hurt, if they were the enemies I should have made for myself by the positions that I took; and they were. I never imagined that anyone gained much in wide popularity—certainly not so much as one lost in relinquishing commitments in favor of easy compromise. If I had to give one word of advice to anyone, it is this: telling the truth exacts no costs, but lying is very expensive, and dissimulation bankrupts. It was in that spirit that I found myself in the middle of the battles in the culture wars and, on some noteworthy occasions, promoted myself from buck private to corporal for a week or so at most.

Let me tell you how it happened. You probably remember the events. In the spring of 1989, war broke out along the Potomac when the public learned that the National Endowment for the Arts had paid big bucks to a sculptor who promptly produced as his work of art a bottle of urine containing a plastic figure of Christ on the cross. Lest anyone miss the point, he called the thing *Piss Christ*. I think it was in April of that year that I received a letter from Tupelo, Mississippi. The American Family Association (based there) wrote to every member of the National Council on the Arts, the advisory council (effectively: the governing body) of the National Endowment for the Arts. The letter was worded in a civil way but contained a bitter complaint about the use of public funds for the defamation of the Christian religion. Since in my public career I make it a practice to answer all reasonably sane letters concerning public policy for which I bear responsibility, I replied, saying something to the effect, "You're absolutely right, such a thing should not have happened."

I made a note to ask about the matter when the council next met. I knew the funds for *Piss Christ* had come from the North Carolina Council on the Arts, a state agency supported by NEA; so the National Endowment's Council had not voted for those funds (small comfort, but at least a mitigating circumstance). I also wrote back to Tupelo that I thought that a government that cannot support religion, or any particular religion, also should not defame religion, or any particular religion. It seemed to me a moderate and reasonable complaint; my reply, I thought, was sympathetic and hopeful.

But within the same span of time, a still more contentious issue exploded, a photographic exhibit at a museum in Philadelphia, supported by a direct NEA grant, which included pictures no TV station could air by reason of their explicit sexual character—the famous Mapplethorpe exhibit. Not personally drawn into the conflict, I checked to see how I had voted, and for what I had voted. It turned out I had voted in favor of "an exhibition of photographs . . ." which showed ingenious and artful use of light and darkness. The staff description of the project contained no hint of the character of what was to be shown. And, all of a sudden, it dawned on me that the NEA staff had denied the council an accurate picture of the project, so that we never knew what we were recommending to the chairman for funding. I said so. And, for a time, I found myself trying to hold against a powerful and zealous extreme the centrist position, corresponding— as I explain later in this book—to the clear consensus of the political community in Washington and throughout the country: no censorship, but also no obscenity through public funds.

That was not the first time I found myself in the trenches. But the other occasions are more economically recorded. In the Jewish community, from college days onward, I have advocated the position that, while we Jewish Americans strongly favor the State of Israel and regard the creation of the Jewish state as one of the greatest historic achievements of the Jewish people, we Jews here are not only Americans; but in the Jewish world, we place an equally high priority on the building, in this country, of a vital and distinct Jewish community here. We are not second-class citizens in the Jewish polity. So I wrote an op-ed piece for the *Washington Post*, saying (in mildly provocative language) that America is our promised land (until the Messiah comes) because it is the best place in the world to be a Jew and practice Judaism. That position, reasonable and centrist, has proved as controversial in the Jewish community as my centrist position on the arts did in the maelstrom of the NEA. Editorial rancor welled up, if not here, then at least there.

In the university I have made my home; it is the only place I have ever wanted to be. When I came to Harvard College in September 1950, I was so taken by the enchanted world I found there that I refused to leave the place for my entire first year, with the odd notion that it might be a Brigadoon, disappearing if I left. I stayed for summer school and held on, graduating in three years and going on to Oxford, then to graduate school (at the Jewish Theological Seminary for education in Judaic sources, then to Columbia University for my Ph.D. in Religion), and pursuing research and teaching—nothing else—for the next three decades. In the university I occasionally took the position, in dramatic, public ways, that the student's best friend is the demanding, insistent professor. I advocated and practiced as a teacher the academic equivalent of tough love.

My devotion to my students takes the form of a

careful hearing of their ideas and a blunt, tough criticism of how they think, what they think, and the way they set down their ideas in writing. Some people value criticism; most do not. A proud and unreconstructed reactionary on the campus, I fought and lost long, often lonely battles for the integrity of learning. And the battles were not with students, but professors. For I told the students that indulgent professors did not love them, and I told the university that there are other, better ways for preserving, enhancing, and transmitting learning, including science. I also informed a once-splendid, small and crafted national research university, which is called Brown, where I taught for twenty-one years, that it had gone to hell and probably could not come back.

These then have formed the arena of a life on the edges of the public place: the academy, the arts, religion, the Jewish religion, in particular. A single set of convictions has guided me in addressing issues as they came along: I believe in God, the sanctity of the human intellect, and the United States of America; the ultimate worth of life, the gift of God; the supremacy of reason and rationality; the non-negotiable condition of civilization; and the unique promise of this country in a world that envies not only our wealth, but also our freedom. In public life on the campus, in the politics of culture, and in the religious dimension of the country's commonwealth, I have stood up and I have been counted (and on more than one occasion, also knocked down and counted out).

The plan of this book is simple. The first three parts—half of the book—focus upon the academy and its failures, because I did and do my service there, so that is where I fight. In an age in which newcomers find a welcome on the campus, only to exclude those already present, I argue for inclusion of new and nurture of the old. In a time in which the received curriculum is dismantled, I remind you that the curriculum of the academy bears the burden of civilization; we can forget what it has taken generations of intellect and treasure to learn, losing access to what we now know. Then, and only then, I turn to the specifics of the campus.

Mine is no merely negative case. I choose writings that not only say what is wrong, but also spell out what I value: how I think teachers should teach and students should learn. I spell out the stakes in university life, pointing out that civilizations have found other means of both educating the young and handing on what they knew. The university as an institution possesses no lien upon the future; it came from somewhere, and it can give way to other means of accomplishing the same necessary goals. I spell out what has gone wrong on the campus and specify where I think the blame must lie.

Since in Part Two I indict the presidents, provosts, deans, and trustees of my time on the scene, in Part Three I move on to the corruption of the professors—their thirst for recognition without achievement, their hunger for the honor conferred, not earned, and their exquisitely sensitive response to the appeal of snobbery. I call attention to two great books of recent times, one not yet accorded proper recognition, and the other deserving of still more praise than it has rightfully received.

From the campus, I proceed to the distinct topics, the Arts Endowment and the arts. These I treat briefly. The institutions of the arts lose touch with the artists; orchestras pay everybody but the musicians well; museums celebrate panache and style, the artists in attendance rarely dressing to the occasion. Trustees of universities rarely read books and never know what professors really do—or much care to find out. My wife is an artist, and through her and her co-workers, I have learned about the curse of grace: having a rare ability that no one rewards. Since my capacities—those of intellect in the academy—bring recognition and rich rewards, the security of tenure, and a comfortable career, I have to call attention to the situation of others, equally possessed of special gifts but not honored or rewarded for the things they do exceedingly well.

Religion in general, and Judaism in particular, has engaged my deepest loyalties. I do not present religion the way the other side advocates atheism and militant secularism; that is, I point to our failures and our flaws. For tension between God who calls and frail humanity's response must always mark out this-worldly presence of the transcendent, which is, after all, organized religion—in churches, mosques, temples, and synagogues. I spell out what seem to me three propositions of general interest: the paradox of religion, the conception that someone can be "religious in general," and the difficulty of coping with the critical, definitive fact of religion in this country—its diversity.

Finally, to Judaism in particular, issues of broad public, even political interest. The Jews form an ethnic group, but Judaism is a religion. How the two hold together or even relate is not always easily sorted out. People use the ethnic adjective, "Jewish," when they mean the religious one, "Judaic," and then define "Judaism" by a public opinion poll of the Jews. But the results obscure the character of the ethnic group and the religion alike, and Gentiles find matters confusing. Here I explain how religion and ethnicity sometimes mix, sometimes keep apart.

Since the Jews form an ethnic group, they appear comparable to Italo- or Irish- or Hispanic- or African-Americans. Since, among the Jews, Judaists practice the religion Judaism, these seem comparable to Roman Catholics or Southern Baptists or Evangelicals. That confusion of the ethnic and the religious is sorted out in the final part of the book. I end with a look to the future: a distinctively Judaic reason to affirm life and oppose death on demand. A third child in a Depression family, I was informed by my mother early on that two would have been enough, but if it had to be a third, then she'd really wanted a girl and would have called her "Jacqueline," so I must be "Jackie." I take abortion personally. The Judaic toast—*le-hayyim*, "to life"—extends to the frontiers of life: no abortion, no euthanasia (in its many forms). That, sum and substance, is what this book concerns: the requirements of a life, in society, of worth and dignity. That is what it means to be "in our image, after our likeness," God's likeness on earth, all of us together.

Acknowledgments

No work of mine can omit reference to the exceptionally favorable circumstances in which I conduct my research. I wrote this book at the University of South Florida, which has afforded me an ideal situation in which to conduct a scholarly life. I express my thanks for not only the advantage of a Distinguished Research Professorship, which must be the best job in the world for a scholar, but also of a substantial research expense fund, ample research time, and some stimulating and cordial colleagues. In the prior chapters of my career, I never knew a university that so prized professors' scholarship and publication and treated with respect the professors who actively pursue research. The University of South Florida, and nine universities that comprise the Florida State University System as a whole, exemplify the high standards of professionalism that prevail in publicly sponsored higher education in the USA. They provide the model that privately sponsored universities would do well to emulate. Here there are rules; achievement counts; and presidents, provosts, and deans honor and respect the University's principal mission: scholarship—scholarship alone both in the classroom and in publication.

Jacob Neusner
Distinguished Research Professor of Religious Studies
University of South Florida Tampa

Prologue

A Christian Nation? We Could Do Worse

I must be the only Jew in the country not outraged by Governor Fordice's innocent pronouncement last year that America is a Christian nation. Everyone else read him to mean, "This, not that." When he said "Christian," they took his meaning to be, "not Jewish." But in his clumsy way, he was trying to say something else altogether. I think we do well to listen to him, even though I too wish he'd made a ritual obeisance to "Judaeo-Christian," so counting me in, or even better, "a religious, a God-fearing nation," including nearly everybody.

What if he'd said, "America is a nation that fears God"? Would that he were right!

And if he'd added, "This country is founded on the belief that we are subject to the justice and mercy of a caring, loving God, to Whom we are responsible," then the 90 percent of the American people who year after year profess to polltakers that they believe in God, and the nearly as high proportions of the population who pray at home or in synagogues, mosques, temples, and churches—all would have answered, "Amen."

In public life, we don't get to take it back, and no one can blame Governor Fordice for not wanting to fall on his sword in the lobby of the Time-Life Building, or at the end of his final interview with the despicable Mike Wallace on "60 Minutes" to jump out the window. Here is a man of good will, and his is a message of personal faith; he did not ask the Congress to adopt a resolution declaring Jesus Christ savior of the world, any more than the Lubovitcher rabbi has asked the White House to stop serving pork (even though in a momentary high, Governor Clinton in a speech in Brooklyn promised just that!).

The advocates of a clear, non-partisan, non-sectarian, non-political public recognition that this, indeed, is a country founded on belief in God address a different issue altogether. First, we believe that, made in God's image and after God's likeness, all humanity possesses inalienable rights to life, liberty, and the right to pursue a happy life. But, absent such a foundation in faith for the conviction of the sanctity of life, we fear a different image altogether—one that, viewing humanity as negotiable, speaks of "ethnic cleansing" or "extermination" when disposing of human beings, who are now compared to dirt or vermin, as in the Serbian and German instances in our times, or in the case of a foetus, to a blob of protoplasm.

Second, we who glory in the religious character of this country look to religion for the source of wisdom, conscience, and concern to sustain this society. For we see national purpose in no other place. Communism once animated lives, but was shown a monstrous fraud. Nazism and fascism hide out in caves in Idaho. Nationalism after the Cold War scarcely registers. Science and learning tell us how to accomplish our goals. But who is to help us identify our task and frame our vocation? We who believe in God have our answer; that is why we pray for guidance and acknowledge hope when it comes.

Third, for Americans, religion really is a native category, a given and fundamental fact of life. That statement rests on the first amendment, which takes as its generative fact that religion is a reality in the life of this country. The first amendment ensures religious freedom from corrupting political privilege; it presents religion with the greatest gift any political document has ever conceived—definitive status as a fact of life.

So if Governor Fordice, speaking of his own religion, wanted to say that he affirms the nourishing strength religion affords in sustaining the social order of the American people, then he has no apologies to make—surely not to the 90 percent of Americans who share his view. And since he did not propose to repeal the first amendment, but wanted only to make certain militant, politically sponsored secularism did not take over as the doctrine and religion of the state, those same people will answer, "Amen."

But the context in which he made his remarks carries with it a different perspective. He addressed Republican leaders, assembled to talk about the future of the party. Right or wrong, he was heard to be saying that the Republican party should identify itself with the Christian majority. And he spoke in a chamber in which conservative, evangelical Christians, sorely provoked by political sponsorship for activities they believe evil and detestable (e.g., abortion or state-subsidized pornography), have organized to turn themselves into a political, empowered entity. So the furor now playing itself out responds not only to the use of exclusive language to express what is, in truth, a profoundly inclusive sentiment, but to the partisan, cacophonous echoes, too.

The conception that religious beliefs and political behavior can or should be kept apart defies the facts of American politics. First, ethnic groups, including white Southerners, commonly identify with distinctive religious systems as well. Teaching in the world of the Southern Baptists (and enjoying the warmth of their community of faith with us, Israel after the flesh), I cannot see Governor Fordice as an undifferentiated white Protestant. Anyone who thinks that Irish or Italian or Mexican can be distinguished, in the context of American ethnic life, from Catholic—or German or Swedish from Lutheran; or Afro-American from Muslim or African Methodist Episcopal; or Armenian from the Armenian Church; or Greek from Greek Orthodoxy—is blind. The ethnic and the religious go together like bagels and cream cheese. So far as our politics is local and ethnic, it also is religious.

Second, even if ethnic and religious were not united, all studies of the relationship between religion and political action have pointed to a single conclusion, which is that religion is a principal variable, indeed an independent variable, in explaining the choices people make. From Gerhart Lenski's 1960 classic, *The Religious Factor*, through the definitive annual studies by Professor Andrew Greeley's National Opinion Research Center, that single consistent result emerges over decades of social study. It follows that while we, of course, keep church apart from state, we cannot hope to keep religion out of politics. Religion defines how people view the world as much as what some of us eat, or do not eat, for breakfast. Any fantasy that the way people worship on Friday, Saturday, or Sunday has no bearing on how they vote on the first Tuesday in November defies reality.

The real political question facing the Right is whether Protestant Christian conservatives wish to include or exclude Jewish, Catholic, or Muslim conservatives; whether white conservatives want to keep out black conservatives; whether, in all, religion is to form an exclusive or an inclusive force on the right. Secular-minded folk will, of course, throw up their hands in horror that I should even raise the question. Obviously, all conservatives will deplore exclusivism; after all, we really do want to get to go to White House receptions again.

But to treat as secular what is, to us believers, a religious question is to repeat the uncomprehending judgment that gave Governor Fordice so much grief this week. I ask a question of religious belief to religious believers, and the answer cannot come out of unbelievers' appeal to tolerance. Maybe God really is telling conservative Evangelicals to take over the country on their own.

In 1863, a movement got underway, in the blood and suffering of the War between the States/Civil War, to declare America a Christian country. Many supposed that in fighting to free the slaves and preserve democracy and the union, the USA was fighting God's fight. Were the troops not singing the apocalyptic words of Moses's vision in Deuteronomy, marching to battle to the tune, "Mine eyes have seen the glory of the coming of the Lord"? Surely, we are on God's side—so God is on our side—and we should now say so by law. That was what some wanted.

In his second inaugural address a month before he was murdered, Abraham Lincoln raised the question, "Whose side is God on?" He answered it with these words: "They both read the same Bible, and they both pray to the same God, and the prayers of neither have been fully answered."

People, with reason, think we religious people are arrogant and exclusive. But the authentic spirit of American religions speaks through Abraham Lincoln, and to be authentically religious is to love God with open arms, so wide open as to embrace others too. Humility marks the faithful—not arrogance. That is why I like to think that if Governor Fordice wants us to be a Christian country, it will be in the spirit of Abraham Lincoln's reverence for God and acknowledgment of God's dominion; for his Christian country will then be my Judaic country. I am inclined to suppose that Buddhist Americans and Hindu Americans; Muslim Americans and Shinto Americans; Native

Americans, who follow the oldest religions of this continent; and also Americans with new religions and with old ones, with African and Latin American religions and Asian ones, as well as Near Eastern and European ones will join him in saying, "Amen." And *at the faith of hope and humility*, secular Americans too should not find reason to take offense.

Chapter 1

The West and the World: Debating the Curriculum

When we argue about what should be taught in schools and colleges, at stake is our conception of the world. For, in education, we transmit not information, but conception. Our theory of the world tells us what we should teach and whom we may ignore.

Debates precipitated by Secretary of Education William Bennett's important criticism of the Stanford curriculum centered upon the inclusion of formerly ignored groups. But how to include Africa, Asia, Latin America, and the Pacific in such a way as to hold the whole together? Merely political arguments against or for affording a full hearing to the neglected parts of the world (Asia and Africa and Latin America, for instance) are beside the point. If Africa, China, and Latin America are important (and they are!), they belong within the curriculum, and if not, then mere institutional politics should not make any difference. But what defines importance? The real question is not how to include everyone, but why to include anyone, East or West. There has to be a single theory of the whole, of what has made the world we propose to explain to the coming generations, and so, to hand on to them.

I think we should continue to lay stress on the West, its history and culture, while encompassing the rest; the West has made the world we know. Anyone who wants to participate in world civilization in the coming century had better know precisely how and why the West has defined, and will continue to define, that civilization. Why do I say so? Because everybody wants what we have, which is science and technology, prosperity, and mass participation in politics—that is, our philosophy, our economics, our politics.

It is the simple fact that science and technology emerge out of Western philosophy, not out of the philosophy of India or China, not out of Africa. India, China, Africa, Latin America—all form part of that one world that we wish the coming generations to understand. At issue in academic debate in the next half-century will be the place of the West in the world. Since, as a matter of fact, everywhere in the world people aspire to those material advantages that flow, uniquely I think, from the modes of social organization that the West has devised—the West's economics, the West's science and technology, and also, let us say it straight out, the West's politics and philosophy, understood as modes of thought and inquiry—I think it is time to stop apologizing and to start analyzing what has made Western civilization the world-defining power that it has become.

Study India, China, Japan, Latin America? Of course. But, what do we want to know? One critical question that demands our study of the rest of the world is simply this: why has the West created what the rest now wants? Why no capitalism in India, China, or Judaism? Why no science in Africa? Why no democracy in Asia? And, conversely, why science and technology, democracy, and economics as a theory of the increase of wealth in the West?

But, to answer those questions, we begin where science, economics, politics, and technology begin and from whence they are diffused, and that is, as a matter of fact, the West, and, to begin with, Western Europe.

When nowadays people rightly want to find a place

in the study of civilization that the academy sustains for Africa, Asia, peoples indigenous to every region and land—we all need to frame a global program of thought and reflection. And, if we are not merely to rehearse the facts of this one and that one, we shall require modes of comparison. That is not a recipe for relativism. It is an invitation to analyze and compare and contrast cultures, all of them honored, each of them placed into relationship with the others. And, the foundations for comparison are laid by those shared and universal concerns represented by economics, politics, and philosophy.

Hence, sustaining questions, applying to all areas because of their ubiquitous relevance, explain why this, not that. Since the simple fact of world civilization is that the West has now defined the world's economy, politics, and philosophy, and since all social systems measure themselves by Western civilization in its capacity to afford to large masses of people both the goods of material wealth and the services of political power, the indicative traits of the West demand close study.

These are, I think, in politics, mass distribution of power in political structures and systems, in economics, capitalism, and in philosophy, the modes of thought and inquiry we call scientific. And, these will dictate the shape of the curriculum, because they adumbrate the structure of world civilization today.

Does that mean we have nothing to learn from Asia, Africa, and Latin America? We have much to learn once we establish our common questions and perspectives. There is no understanding the world without the West, and there is no understanding the rest of the world without grasping the relationship of the West and its unique achievements in science, economics, politics, and philosophy with the rest of the world.

So, no, not everything is as important as everything else, and, yes, some things are going to receive more attention than others, and, indeed, it is not a matter of counting noses. West is not best, but there are things about the West that matter everywhere, and those are the traits of Western civilization that join the study of the West with learning about the rest. In composing a curriculum addressed to world civilization in economics, politics, and philosophy, we shall hold together East and West, South and North, and, it goes without saying, both genders as well. There *can* be a curriculum once we recognize that there really is a single world civilization, important to us all.

Democracy, capitalism, anti-colonialism, science, technology, ever-rising productivity in industry and agriculture—these deeply Western and, as a matter of fact, quintessentially American values are now universal. And, they define what there is to know about everyone, everywhere—beginning, of course, with ourselves.

Chapter 2

Can Humanity Forget What It Knows?

Civilization hangs suspended, from generation to generation, by the gossamer strand of memory. If only one cohort of mothers and fathers fails to convey to its children what it has learned from its parents, then the great chain of learning and wisdom snaps. If the guardians of human knowledge stumble only one time, in their fall collapses the entire edifice of knowledge and understanding. More important, therefore, than finding new things is sifting and refining the received truths. And the generation that will go down through time bearing the burden of disgrace is not the one that has said nothing new—for not much new marks the mind of any age—but the one that has not said what is true.

These self-evident truths concerning the continuity of civilization pertain not alone to wisdom, such as what philosophy and religion preserve. They address much more concrete matters than the wise conduct of affairs. There are things that we know because of the hard work of people who have come before, knowledge that we have on account of other people's trial and error. And that is knowledge that also hangs in the balance from age to age, knowledge that we can and do forget, with awful consequences for those who will come after us, to whom we, for our part, are answerable.

The simple fact is that we either remember or we recapitulate the work of finding out—one or the other. And now, with 5,000 years of recorded science and philosophy, mathematics, history and social science, literature and music and art—if we lose it all, we probably shall never regain what is gone. It would be too much work, require resources of time and intellect not likely to come to hand. Lest my meaning be lost in abstraction, let me give a single concrete case. When the turret of the battleship *Iowa* suffered an explosion, people could not repair it. The reason is that the materials and technological know-how to repair the guns, available when the ship was built in World War II, were lost beyond recovery. That is what I mean when I say civilization hangs suspended by fragile strands, indeed. So too, when people decided to resume construction of the Cathedral of St. John the Divine in New York City, people found out that only a few stone masons were left in the world who could work the giant blocks from which a cathedral is built; they could train young apprentices, or the work would not be done. Languages, too, have come and gone; someone once told me of meeting the last person in the world who spoke Cornish as a native language; and linguists make haste to preserve what is nearly going to be lost as an example of the potentialities of intelligible speech.

I owe this point to a biologist at Rutgers University, David Ehrenfeld, writing in *Orion* (Autumn 1989, 5-7), who argues that "loss of knowledge and skills is now a big problem in our universities." That is a problem, he maintains, not in the humanities, which we know are dying, but in the natural sciences. His case in point is one that surprised me. He says, "We are on the verge of losing our ability to tell one plant or animal from another and of forgetting how the known species interact among themselves and with their environments." This is because subjects fall out of the curriculum, or are taught piecemeal by people on the periphery of the university. He says, for example, of "Classification of Higher Plants," "Marine Invertebrates," "Ornithology," "Mammalogy," "Cryptograms" (ferns and mosses), "Biogeography," "Comparative Physiology" that "you may find some of them in the catalogue, but too often with the notation along side, 'not offered. . . .'" Ehrenfeld explains: "The features that distinguish lizards from snakes from crocodilians from turtles . . . aren't any less accepted or valid than they were twenty-five years ago, nor are they easier than they used to be to learn on your own from books without hands-on laboratory instruction." But people do not work on those fields.

Ehrenfeld further explains why the question is an urgent one. He tells the following story: "One morning last April, at eight o'clock, my phone rang. It was a former student of mine who is now a research endocrinologist at a major teaching hospital in Houston. She had an odd question: at what point in animal evolution was the hemoglobin molecule first adopted for use specifically as an oxygen carrier? It was an essential piece of information for medical research she was planning." The information the student wanted was in an elementary "introduction to comparative biochemistry." When Ehrenfeld asked colleagues who was working on this sort of thing, he found out nobody. The graduate students had never even heard of the field of comparative biochemistry.

Now here we have a very concrete case of the loss of knowledge once possessed. Ehrenfeld comments: "Not outdated, not superseded, not scientifically or politically controversial, not even merely frivolous: a whole continent of important human knowledge gone." It was not dead; it lived only in books, which no one read or understood or could use in the quest for knowledge. Ehrenfeld draws from this story conclusions that need not detain us. In his view, the loss of comparative biochemistry is because of the flow of funds into the wrong hands, into the hands of people who are not "capable of transmitting our assembled knowledge of the natural world to the next generation." So he says, "I fear for conservation when there is no one left in our places of learning who can tell one moth from another, no one who knows the habits of hornbills, no one to puzzle over the diversity of hawthorns."

If we now take the case as exemplary, we may ask ourselves, "Where in society do we assign the task of holding on to what we know and of making sure the next generation gains access to that?" The stakes are too high for the answer to invoke the episodic and the anecdotal: "Here am I; send me." The accident of individuals finds its match in the uncertainty of books; putting whatever is worth knowing into books, encyclopedias for example, will not serve, since mere information does not inform; and facts without explanation of what they mean and how they fit together do not bear meaning or serve a purpose. In age succeeding age, in some few places, the mind of humanity in the past is recreated, not preserved inert, but actively replicated, re-enacted as a model for the mind of humanity to come. I speak, of course, of schools as those few places, of teachers as the actors out of knowledge in intellectually replicable form. For to preserve what we know, we must repeat the processes of discovery, since the only mode of really learning is our own discovery, which permits us not merely to know things, but to understand something. All the facts in the world about moths and hornbills and hawthorns, left uninterpreted, will not yield comparative biochemistry.

As it happens, I have spent my life working on a document that is composed so as to present, within a few volumes, the life and structure, the way of life and world view and social theory, of an entire world of humanity: the Jewish people. A few remarkable intellectuals undertook to write a book that would serve as not a mere source of information but as a handbook of civilization: how to form society, what society had to know to do its work—all of useful knowledge so formed as to yield meaning and order and coherence: the deep structure of a social being. To write a book to do that, they worked out not an encyclopedia of information, but a guide book for a journey of mind, of intellect: this is how to think, this is what to think, this is why to think. They made certain therefore that what they knew would be known by coming generations, not because the institutions would endure, nor because the politics would accord to their doctrines priority of place. Indeed, the writers of this document would have found surprising Professor Ehrenfeld's certainty that problems are to be solved by putting money in the right hands, or keeping it out of the wrong ones.

What they did was two things. First, they wrote a book that could be sung. Second, they wrote notes to the music, so that anyone could sing the song. They did not spell out everything; rather they gave signals of how, if you wanted to spell things out, you could on your own do so: don't ask, discover. So, they opened the doors of learning to make place for all to come; learning served then as an active verb, with discovery its synonym. These notes—signals of how a moving argument would be reconstructed, how reason might be recapitulated—were few, perhaps not the eight notes of our octave, but not an infinite repertoire of replicable sounds, either. But the medium—notes to the music—is only secondary. Their primary insight into how civilization, as they proposed to frame it, should be shaped lay in another matter altogether. It had to do with their insistence upon the urgency of clear and vigorous and rigorous thought, the priority of purpose to argument, and the demand for ultimate seriousness about things to be critically examined. Through practical reasoning and applied logic, they formed the chains to link mind to mind, past to future, through a process that anyone could enter—and no one, once in, would leave.

I said they wrote a book that could be sung. I mean that both literally, in that, their writing was a document meant to be said out loud, not read silently; meant to be studied in community through debate, not meditated upon privately and personally; writing that was, in the old and classic sense, political—public, shared, subject to coercion, if in the form of reason, rather than naked power, to be sure. But I mean that in another sense, as well. The great author James Baldwin said in a short story that every song begins in a cry. So when I say they wrote a book that could be sung, I meant to invoke the metaphor of a piece of writing that begins not with the words and the music, but in the guts, a piece of writing that is thought before thinking, insight before application and explication, attitude and emotion prior to their reformulation in propositions formed of words. I speak of revelation such as most of us have known and of which all of us have heard: the unearned insight, the unanticipated moment of understanding. That is what I mean by a book that could be sung, of truth in a form of such art that whoever hears will see and feel and know in a knowledge that is defining.

So if it is possible to forget what we have learned, leaving for a coming generation the task of recapitulating processes of discovery and interpretation, it also is possible to imagine and even identify the means by which, as a matter of fact, humanity has defended itself from the loss of what it already has in hand. If I use the Talmud, on which I work, as a case in point, others may well identify other appropriate cases. I think of such fields as music and mathematics, philosophy and its offspring in the social sciences, and a variety of the natural sciences as well, as fields of learning that link us to the accumulated treasures of important knowledge and sustaining truth. What they have in common is rules of right thought, a heritage of conventions to be replicated, retested, and realized from age to age, a process of testing and re-evaluation, an endless openness to experiment, whether in the laboratory or in thought. Indeed, much that we in universities identify as useful and important knowledge qualifies. For, as a matter of fact, so far as the sum of human knowledge is concerned, either we in universities will convey it to the coming generation, or it will be lost for all time.

It is the simple fact that nearly everything that we teach in universities comes to us from somewhere else, and most of it comes to us from generations of intellects long ago. Whether philosophy or mathematics or music, whether how we regain the past in history, or how we interpret the facts of the natural world, the treasure and storehouse of human knowledge are realized today, in the here and now, in universities—or those treasures are lost, much as comparative biochemistry formed a threatened species of learning when people lost access to what that field had to tell them. So the task of universities, if not unique then at least distinctive among all of the institutions that preserve and hand on past to future, is to preserve civilization and to afford access to civilization. Ours is the task of remembering, recapitulating, re-enacting. Ours is the task of reminding, in a very odd sense of the word, that is, to re-gain mind. We form the links in the great chain of learning, and if we prove strong to the task, another generation will know what we do; but if we prove weak, the work of many generations past will be lost, and many generations to come will be the losers. The stakes in universities and what they do, therefore, are not trivial; we do more than serve; we carry out more than a transient or merely useful task. We preserve in a very special way: we show the generation to come the how of knowledge, not merely the what; we show in our time what humanity has done over all time to make sense of the world.

Lest these observations on the nature of knowledge, the danger of forgetting what we know, appear mere commonplaces, let me point out alternative views. For I set forth a profoundly conservative theory of universities and their tasks, based on a deeply conservative premise on the character of civilization and society. I do maintain that it is more difficult to keep what we have than to add to what we know. I very much take to heart Professor Ehrenfeld's warning that if the few old men who know how to work the giant blocks of stone die without heirs, we shall no longer know how to build cathedrals; and in time to come, when we see them, we shall not even know what they are, in the way that when we see the monstrous statues on Easter Island, we do not know what they are.

Then the failure of civilization, the forgetting of what we know, looms large in my mind: we can lose what we have but get nothing better. Society defines what is at stake, and risking its slender goods for the main chance threatens utter chaos: "gone, not outdated, not superseded, not even controversial, not frivolous: a whole continent of important human knowledge gone!" Indeed, so far as civilization finds nourishment in knowledge and understanding—and I cannot define civilization without knowledge and understanding—there can be no greater catastrophe than that loss of a continent of human knowledge; that clod that washes out to sea is all the ground we ever had on which to make sense of something.

What then, we must ask ourselves, does the fact that humanity indeed can forget what it now knows dictate for public policy in the here and now? The stakes having been defined in the way I have, the upshot is not to be gainsaid.

First, our principal task in universities must be the work of rigorous teaching. At stake in our class room is the coming generation and its capacity to know and make sense of things. Therefore, our main effort focuses upon the how of learning, by which I mean upon how our students grasp what we wish to tell them, on the processes by which we turn information into useful knowledge, useful knowledge into understanding—all through (re)discovery, the recreation of intellect in age succeeding age.

The corollary, second, is that the creation of new knowledge is less important than the recapitulation of received knowledge. Most professors, most of the time in most universities, know little about what it means to create new knowledge. As a matter of fact, it is estimated that two-thirds of all professors have published scarcely a line; of those who publish books, most publish one, few more than one, which means the discovery of new knowledge in the responsible form of a statement for the criticism of others ends with the dissertation; and, so I hear, 95 percent of all scholarly books come from perhaps 5 percent of the scholars. What this means is that most professors, most of the time in most universities, find themselves expected to do what few of them have ever done, and few still have done more than once. We have therefore to reconsider the entire structure of higher education, and our task is to reframe our work in such a way that the work people really do—and want to do and often do supremely well—is valued, and that that work is done. Most professors should teach more than they now do, but they also should study more than they now do in order to teach what they themselves have made their own.

Third, the recapitulation of received knowledge is not the same thing as the mere repetition of things people think they know, or have heard from others assumed to know what they are talking about. Teaching is now defined in some few, conventional ways. For example, the teacher talks; the students listen. The teacher is the authority, the students inert and passive respondents thereto. Or opinions are exchanged, so that no one is an authority, and there is no task but to say what one thinks. For another example, students listen to professors, but not to one another, and professors listen to no one but themselves. For a third example, writing lots of things down on paper is taken to demonstrate knowledge and understanding. But what if teaching is understood in other terms altogether, as engagement in a shared task of learning and understanding and explanation? What if teaching is a form of leading, specifically of leading by example—follow me! That is, to be sure, a risk-laden mode of teaching, and it is a way of teaching that fails much more often than it succeeds. For it makes the teacher into the model—the example rather than the authority, and models or examples are there to be examined and criticized. And that mode of teaching makes the class room into a laboratory in which mental experiments are undertaken. Since in this reading of the act of teaching, the professors turn out to be the guinea pigs, my call is for us to play a not very inviting role. But it is an honest one, and it is one that serves.

Fourth and last, if, as I claim, our task is to echo the natural sounds of knowledge, which are knowledge, then some sounds will resonate, others not. Today, of course, we make a cacophony of noise; most of what we teach is mere facts, about this and that, and no theory instructs us on what takes precedence and why some facts are trivial or merely particular. For example, entire areas of learning even now turn out to be made up of an endless series of cases—this, that, and the other thing, yielding no theory, generated by no theory: pointless information—or cases that yield no truth to speak of. One such field is ethics; you can study journalistic ethics, medical ethics, legal ethics, you can even raise money for professorships in all of these subjects. And you can make yourself into an expert on some field of ethics, medical ethics having attracted more than its share of failed careerists and bright-eyed opportunists than any other field of learning in the 1980s, much the counterpart of social science in the 1950s, or computer science in the 1970s. But these entrepreneurs of learning, trained in one thing and doctors of everything, make things up as they go along, for what sounds right is right; there is no theory of the thing they study because there is no principled inquiry into the foundations of analysis and criticism. Yet we in the West have inherited a tradition of philosophical ethics that comes to us from the Greeks and a tradition of theological ethics that comes to us from ancient Israel through Christianity and Judaism; we have those theories, those principles of decision making, that have laid the foundations for coherent thinking about a cogent subject. When a field can give only examples and cases, its casuistry attests to its intellectual bankruptcy. The field of medical ethics, as currently practiced, exemplifies better than any other presently current why, when civilization perishes, charlatans prosper. But the casuistry serves because philosophy is not learned, and reinventing the wheel, the ethicists in the hospitals unwittingly teach a dreadful lesson indeed: what it means to lose what you've got.

So, yes, humanity can forget what it knows, and that is so in biology and philosophy, and the costs are there to see at Easter Island or in the shelves of books we no longer can read but need to read, and in the areas of learning that are true and useful but no longer accessible. The task is not new knowledge but the reconsideration of knowledge. When we succeed—and we in universities are the only one who can do the work—we shall hold on to what we have received, because we shall have made it our own. And that is what I conceive to be the principal work of any generation: to make what has come to us as a gift into something that is our own, that is, something that we too can use; in the case of learning, I mean, to make learning our own in such a way that we too can learn.

Chapter 3

What Went Wrong on the Campus

A whole generation of university professors now moves into the final decade of their careers. People who earned their doctorates in the 1950s and 1960s now reach their late fifties and sixties, and it is clear, a dramatic change in the composition and character of university faculties will mark the beginning of the next century. We leave the universities as considerably smaller and less consequential places than they were when we came on the scene. But I should claim that we have done our best.

Professors were the earliest victims of the Cultural Revolution of the 1960s, but we went willingly to the barricades, being willing victims. We were the ones to make our peace with what we should have fought. Many of us from that time onward were to witness in our unfolding careers the transformation of the academic world from its gentle and intellectual character—women and men of curiosity, seeking understanding—to something quite different, rather more political and less engaged by learning and teaching.

We have seen the presidents and provosts and deans seek success, not in education, but in public relations, substituting for an academic vision of education an essentially instrumental program of public policy and the shaping of public opinion. We have witnessed the destruction of a beautiful and precious moment in the history of learning. What good has come from the ruin of the old, I do not know. Ours was the transitional generation. We did our best to cope and accommodate, but we received from our masters universities that were better than those we now hand on to our disciples—more humane, more intellectual, of a purer academic character. Our careers have spanned interesting times. But at least, for good or ill, we always knew it. And, for my part, I always said so. At least the other side, from the Cultural Revolution onward, cannot say they did not know what they were doing: they knew precisely what they were doing, and they did it. But I say, "Forgive them Lord, for knowing, they knew not." And forgive us, too, our incapacity to educate.

And yet if truth be told—and I am a truth-teller, it being too costly to me not to tell the truth as I see it—all that has mattered in my life and career, excluding the life of home and family, is book-writing. My advice to the next generation of scholars is that all that matters is the books you write, that alone. For intellect is shaped, where it is accessible, in books, there alone. And we live and strive for the life of mind, for that above all. I wasted much of my life by placing my highest priority upon teaching students and upon engagement with my university. I could have done much more had I understood what lasts and what matters and what makes a difference to the coming age and ages beyond counting, and it is only books, there alone: there alone is life. So I need not mourn the waste of a once precious organization, the university, nor do I mourn the destruction of a once vital institution of society, the one that pays my salary even now, nor do I look back with satisfaction on years given over to students and their nurture. All this is nothing. All that matters lies now in the reader's hand or, at least, sits on the library shelf for readers to come. But that suffices to make this life, my life, worth

What Went Wrong on the Campus

having lived. Let me now spell out why I think the world has lost something of value, and something not very readily replaced.

We shaped our careers to serve three causes: scholarship, teaching, collegial citizenship. We deemed success the writing of books, the raising up of a new generation of thoughtful students, and the sharing of common responsibilities in the building of a campus community of intellect and heart. We measured success by our capacity to contribute to knowledge in some specific way, to share knowledge with others, both in writing and in the class room, and to learn from others and join with others in a common life of intellect. We did not succeed all the time or even very often. But these formed the royal way, the golden measure: scholarship and learning, teaching and sharing, citizenship and caring. It was a gracious ideal, a nourishing and giving and caring faith of the academy and in the academy. We formed that faith not within our own minds alone, but in what we saw in the generation that had brought us up.

If people today wish to conduct research and scholarship, in our day and society, most can do it only in universities or colleges. There is no living to be made outside of the academy in most academic fields. True, in engineering and many of the hard sciences and mathematics, you can hope to pursue research not supported by teaching—hence as a professor in a college—but supported in research institutes, corporations, government, and the like. In the social sciences, sociology, political science, and economics, for example, there are research institutes. But, without inherited money, on a full-time, life-long basis, one cannot study Greek and Roman literature, or medieval history, or English literature, or religion, or any other of the humanities, without a Ph.D. and work as a college professor.

The things we thought mattered when our generation came on the scene—scholarship, publication, teaching in an engagement with students' minds, commitment to excellence in our campus—these no longer find a place on the campus. Universities have become places of privilege and self-indulgence, in which boredom—the cost of easy tenure based on considerations of politics, not accomplishment—reigns, and energy and commitment to learning defy the norm. Tenure marks not achievement but acceptability, and those who go along get along. The road to success is withdrawal and disengagement. As in prison, so in a professorial career: you do your own time. But here our successors, like ourselves, locate themselves by choice—because it is where you can do things you think worth doing, and for that reason you accept the restrictions of the place.

When we came along, the things that mattered in the university were scholarship, teaching, collegiality. If therefore you wanted to teach and also pursue scholarship, you were wise to follow a path to a professorship. You would not get rich, and not much, beyond learning, would ever be at stake. But you would learn and teach and enjoy the satisfactions of accomplishment in teaching others through both classroom engagement and also published scholarship, and those accomplishments would enjoy appreciation among colleagues. Today the gentle virtues of learning give way to more robust values of politics and management. If young people want to teach, there are better places in which to do it than colleges. If they want to pursue scholarship as an exercise in on-going curiosity, in many fields there are better opportunities, and more agreeable situations, than universities. It comes down to this: if you have to use universities in order to conduct a career of learning, then use them.

Today for those who wish to sustain scholarship, universities offer one opportunity—and perhaps the only one. Universities two generations ago were not the main or the only medium for scholarship, and many of the great discoveries in the humanities and sciences from the Enlightenment to our own century did not come from people who held professorships. People drawn by curiosity found ways to make a living—or lived on inherited wealth—and pursued their scholarship. Darwin and Freud—to name two of the greatest intellects we have known—pursued their research without university support. And many of the most important ideas that now shape minds came from people who made their living other than through university teaching—and some of them did not even have doctorates. Yet they made their discoveries and gained a hearing for their ideas. Today, much research, even when conducted in universities, finds support other than through students' tuition. That is the reason, the only reason, for seeking employment in colleges and universities, as we now know them. For they have ceased to be communities, and they are, in the main, not very academic.

Why has it come to this? Let me explain how things were the way they were—and why they changed. We who began in the 1950s and saw the 1960s as assistant professors and the 1970s and 1980s as the senior faculty and now move toward our final decades of teaching and publishing research took over the dream of an earlier generation and lived through the nightmare of our own times. Our model of the university came to us as the gift of the generation of the Second World War, which brought America to a position of responsibility within the larger world. Universities took on the work of educating young Americans to address that great world beyond. Professors became scholars, not only teachers, responsible for learning more and more about many more things. To do our work, professors had both to learn new things and also to teach worthwhile ones, and students, for their part, had actually to study. Demanding, serious times awaited. No longer Mr. Chipps, benign but boring, saying over and over again the lessons he had learned from the Mr. Chipps who had come before. And no more place for the cheering and the singing and the gentleman's C.

What changed? It was the entire configuration of higher education. Colleges became universities, and universities turned themselves into centers of research. Publication mattered. Tenure came to those who produced. Students studied, scholars taught, knowledge expanded and exploded; higher education in America set the standard for the world, as much as German universities had defined the golden measure a century earlier—and with good reason. From our universities came the sciences and the scientists, the social science, the humanities revived by fresh questions, the spirit of discovery, the compelling call of vivid curiosity.

In 1950, at the age of eighteen I went to Harvard, because so far as I then knew, it was the only university in which research went on. (Of course, I was wrong, but for an adolescent intellectual in West Hartford, Connecticut, the choices were Harvard, Yale, and Brown, and among them, only Harvard seemed a place where people read books.) But ten years later, a dozen New England universities, and many score throughout the country, had gained that ambition to transform and transcend; that in the aggregate formed the great leap forward of America's universities. A new definition of the calling of higher education took hold. We were partners, all of us on the campus, in an adventure of learning. That meant that students would study, not merely gain credentials. Scholars would publish, not merely speculate. Teachers would conduct the class room as a realm of discovery, not merely as a stage for the rehearsal of other peoples' knowledge and the professor's opinions of that knowledge. Knowledge itself—the definition of what is to be learned for the degree of Bachelor of Arts or of Science—vastly changed. Old boundaries gave way. New subjects found entry.

That was the vision. Along with the best and the brightest I knew, I was drawn to a life of learning: reading and writing, studying and teaching, speculating and testing propositions: what if? and why? and why not? That was the life I chose, and given the choice again and the years in which to carry it out, I should choose that same life again. But not for the same reasons, and not in the same realm of reality. Our tide flowed in, in the 1950s and 1960s. But, it flowed out again. The ebb-tide came in the late 1960s and early 1970s. We who then were young, the legacy of the vision of the 1940s and 1950s, sustained the hope that others had given us but confronted a world no one could earlier have conceived. The great presidents of the 1950s and 1960s were scholars, one and all. They also had the capacity to find the money they needed to build their universities by finding greatness in scholarship. They also were educators, who framed success by the criterion of the quality of mind—and in the colleges, even the character and conscience—of the young people for whom, for four years, they and their faculties bore responsibility.

But in the trials of social revolution and political crisis, when the campus became the battlefield and the college students the shock troops, the scholars and the educators failed and were replaced. What most of them could not, and did not, do was hold the center. They were educators, scholars and teachers, not politicians, not managers, not planners of budgets and manipulators of women and of men. And others came along—people thought they were needed—who could do those things. We who are still on the campus pay the price of the campus revolution of the 1960s and 1970s. And why not? Ours was the mistake, for we believed when we should have doubted, and we thought we could, by an act of the faculty senate, change human nature, reform society, and redeem the world. But we could not even save ourselves and our own ideals when the barbarians came. And come they surely did.

University leadership had now found its definition, but not in the particular requirements of the tasks of the academy: scholarship and research. Now what the campus needed was what other large institutions—deemed no different from the university in substance, only in form—also needed. A person with political capacities could move from the cabinet or the House of Representatives to the campus. A general could turn himself into a college president. So could a chief executive officer of a large corporation. So could a fund-raiser, a foundation program officer, anybody who had shown capacities to control, manage, administer—and it did not matter what. These new types of academic office-holders were not chosen because of achievement in education and scholarship, and they did not value the capacity to teach and to write—things they had never done and could not do. They were chosen to keep the peace and balance the budget, much as the Lord-Mayor of Johannesburg can keep the peace and balance the budget. And that is what they did.

The ideal of the builders of the 1940s and 1950s produced us, the professors of the 1960s, into the twenty-first century. We received a vision, and we lived by it. The vision discerned a different America and demanded of the academy a distinctive calling. But the academy can yet serve useful purposes, if not the cause of education and citizenship, community and civil discourse, or reasoned argument about honorable alternatives. So use it for what it can give: the chance to do your work, that alone. The academy has no room any more for those who find themselves called to learning and to service. It is a place for careers—and careerists. It is not going to change very soon. So if the university serves your purpose, use it. Take your pay and do your job, just as you would in any other corporation, in a normal, utterly professional, and impersonal transaction. More is not wanted.

But learning will go forward, if not on the campus, then elsewhere. For the curiosity of humanity draws us onward, and if this kind of institution does not nurture learning, some other will. The will to know, to ask why, and why not, and what if?—that never-to-be-satisfied hunger and thirst will never fail us but will always sustain us. It is what it means to be human. If I had to do it all over again, would I give my life to learning and teaching, sharing and building? Yes, I would do precisely what I did with my life: get learning, pursue learning. But I would do it for different reasons, and I would do it in a different way.

I would do it for one reason only, which is, as I said, because if you want to be a scholar, you have to make a living, and for many subjects, you can make a living as a scholar only in a university. And I would do it not as I have done, giving half of my energy and commitment to students, and half to scholarship. I would give all of my energy and commitment to scholarship, and leave over only what I absolutely had to reserve for a minimal accomplishment of such tasks of teaching as I could not decently avoid.

So my best wisdom for the next generation, as just now it begins work for the Ph.D. and a life of learning:

[1] Scholarship, in published form, is all that matters in graduate school and in your career beyond. Pay no attention, now or later on, to issues of higher education and the larger setting of the university. These should not concern you.

[2] Do not think of yourself as an educator, let alone as a teacher, but only as a scholar. If you have to make a living in the academy, teach as little as you can, to as few students as you can, and avoid all engagement with students. And, for the rest, no committees, no politics, no involvements, just read and write.

[3] Take from the university what it has to give you, but give nothing more than your scholarship, which is to say, nothing the university wants or values. Leave the university to those who wish today to make of it what they will: the presidents, provosts, and deans, on the one side, and the students who come and go, on the other. They will do as they like anyhow, so keep out of their way and do your work. Use them as they use you, and you will have a useful career—for yourself and for your field of learning; and these are all that matter.

Chapter 4

"The Malpractice in Education Act" and Other Suggestions for Reform

The ruined state of many, though by no means most, universities shows the cost of not calling to account the malefactors of great academic power in the past generation—the presidents, provosts, and deans who used power to please personal prejudice or mere whim and ignored the public interest. For in no less a way than the physicians who botch operations or the financiers who steal the pensions of old men and women, the presidents of the last ten or fifteen years should be called to account. For example:

- the president of Stanford, who billed whatever he wanted to "overhead costs" paid for by federal funds (now estimated at just short of half a billion dollars!);
- the president of the University of South Carolina, who used public funds for off-budget purposes (and pinched the behinds of his male assistants);
- the administration of Yale University, which for a decade or more, balanced the budget by postponing needed maintenance of its buildings and now has to fire professors to find a billion dollars to repair falling walls and leaky roofs;
- the trustees and administration of the University of Bridgeport, which got their school into such a mess it has to close or sell out to the Moonies;

- the president, provost, and deans of Syracuse University, who miscalculated their budgets by so many millions that the future of the place is in doubt;
- the last president of Brown University, who raised millions and wasted the money on a gaggle of glitzy new programs utterly irrelevant to the academy, and who—in an astounding administrative calamity—lost (among other assets) six of eighteen professors of a once-great mathematics department just by not answering mail from the chairman.

The list goes on, but the point is simple. Decisions made by quite ordinary people simply ruined the universities for which they bear responsibility. Should they not be called to account for their actions and venal policies, as much as doctors or lawyers can be sued for malpractice, or business people for fraud?

In fact, what they did to the academy they held in trust was worse than medical malpractice. For doctors can make honest mistakes. But in the academy, these people were warned but went ahead doing whatever they felt like doing that morning (which not seldom involved ruining the professors who warned them).

Now that alumni sue universities for failing to educate, so moving us rapidly toward that much needed "pure food and drug act" for university advertising (than which there is no more deceitful advertising in the market today), surely it is time for someone to say, "Well there is good and bad in academic administration—and there is also culpability."

Not everyone is to blame. Some clearly stupid decisions are not culpable; you can't sue for stupidity, even the idiocy of dismantling a small, classy research-oriented "university college," such as Brown's great presidencies created from 1937 to 1966. A bad decision is not a venal one, and a lot of people decided excellence and academic achievement are not wanted at Brown—mediocre professors happily concurred.

But what about the sheer maladministration involved, for example, in a board of trustees that simply refuses to look and listen?

Successive heads of Brown's trustees, to take one example, shrugged off senior professors' warnings and didn't ask the tough questions to their glitzy president in time to stop the silliness.

And where were the trustees of Yale when they should have walked around the campus and noticed that the buildings were falling down?

And how come the trustees of Stanford didn't read the budget once in a while? These people were stupefied by the honor of being trustees, fearful of jeopardizing their personal glory by making waves. So they didn't, and their ships sank.

And don't think that it was the same everywhere, far from it. Presidents, provosts, deans, and trustees that excuse themselves by saying everybody did it (or didn't do it) close their eyes to the competition. And, in higher education, as much as anywhere else, there is plenty of competition.

When Brown was squandering its money on glitz (with all the money spent on International Relations, does anybody think Brown now competes with Johns Hopkins or Georgetown or Tufts?) and losing its great departments' stars, someone else out there was spending money judiciously and picking up the falling stars—and fast. When some presidents spent their universities into oblivion, others more prudential and also smarter were worried about the future—and did something about it.

The acting president of Brandeis a year ago warned me, "We could be the first Eastern Airlines of higher education." But he also worried enough to turn the place around, so far as he could, in his brief tenure. He thought it might close by January 1992, so he told me, but it hasn't, and it won't.

The trustees of New York University kept close watch on the place, not only its budget but also (even) its excellence. And as Columbia sinks into bankruptcy, NYU rises in solvency—and in academic quality.

Many, many state universities—the entire Florida State University system, for instance, struggling with budget crunches long before the privates saw any problems—have already made the tough choices not only to save what's good but even to make stellar appointments. For where do you think the falling stars have been landing?

Florida's state system found the tens of millions needed to outbid MIT for a major scientific research project, winning it for FSU, and that was not an accident, but great leadership and rigorous management from the governor and legislature through the regents and on down into every campus administration. But then the state systems are answerable to the governor and legislature—who are answerable to the voters. The private trustees are answerable to their own consciences, more forgiving judges, not to say suborned juries.

We protect patients from medical malpractice and clients from legal malpractice. We defend investors against insider trading and retirees' pension funds from outright thievery. Aren't universities worthy of protection too? It's time to call to account the presidents, provosts, deans, and trustees, whose malpractice over the past decades has ruined once-great universities. And, when we do, we shall also recognize the presidents and trustees who, in the same period, brilliantly responded to the challenges of the times and turned crisis into opportunity. It's time to write the Malpractice in Education Act of 1992—and pass it.

Now for some suggestions for reform when the new leadership takes over. I begin with a simple fact. In twenty years, not a single important step in defining the tasks of universities has been taken. We professors in general, and at Brown in particular, go through the motions of curricula that have yet to prove their value.

Our policy here at home is simple: Do whatever you want. Take this, or that, or nothing very much. We require no courses but only a major, and while extreme, we at Brown do signal the failure of purpose and the absence of goals that characterize higher education in the two decades beyond the deluge.

But where to start? After twenty years of asking, it is time to find some answers.

Higher education finds its definition in the answers to three questions: [1] who teaches? [2] what? [3] to whom?

Twenty years of dismantling the received programs and familiar purposes of colleges and universities were focused on politics and personalities, that is, answering Nos. 1 and 3. Curiously, the other side—the sorts of people who have been in control of universities for twenty years—have had slight interest in [2]—what is taught.

That then is their weak point; they know full well whom they want to teach and who is to do the teaching. They cannot explain what is to be taught or why it is to be taught. In a strategy of sustained assault upon the pointless melange of topics and purposeless information that today stands behind the baccalaureate degree, we begin the work of reconstruction that is not only urgent, but also timely.

For twenty years, the revolutions of the late 1960s have yielded not a single important educational idea, not a single well-crafted curriculum. The curriculum debate at Stanford found contending parties unable to appeal to shared conceptions of education; the whole focused around issues of politics, not learning. The universities have simply gone through the motions of a received pattern barely grasped and scarcely understood. We who wish to restore and renew the traditions of learning that made universities important to society have the curriculum pretty much to ourselves.

For after all, ideas are power, and we, who value

intellect still and always will, value what people think and the reasons for why they think it. What that means in concrete terms is that we have to ask the fundamental questions: What do we teach? Why do we teach this subject, not that subject? How is a young person's life enhanced, changed, in particular, through learning and through intellectual things?

For people send their children to costly universities that give courses and so claim that learning things matters. The degree is gained not by charm or public service or interesting hobbies but by solid achievement in the class room and laboratory and library, achievement tested and measured by examination and critical scrutiny.

Then by our own word, we in universities allege that, in the maturing of young people, what we teach plays a considerable role—one so critical that parents and society should devote scarce resources to our work with students. But if we cannot explain what we teach and why and provide an account of a well-crafted education, then our word is worthless.

But if we claim that we have a solid message to impart, where to start? It is with a sustained attack on the anti-intellectual view that everything is right and that we cannot make judgments as to what is true and what is not true. In the two decades in which no one cared about what was taught but only about who did the teaching to whom, the universities have surrendered to relativism. That is the view that everything is right for someone, depending on context, and nothing is ever wrong everywhere and all the time.

Accordingly, one subject is as good as the next, one opinion as the next, one act as the next. That has meant universities could not lay claim to reason as arbiter of truth, experiment as test of knowledge, sustained critical inquiry as purposeful in finding out what is so and what is not.

And, that accounts for the utter incapacity of the

leadership of twenty years to deal with the curriculum. If you don't know what is true and what is untrue, then what difference does it make whether you teach this or that or the other thing? Everything is equally worthwhile (or worthless). And, all that for eighteen thousand dollars a year!

Indeed on the campus as we know it, just as the universities cannot tell you what is true and what is false, so they cannot tell you who is sane and who is having emotional problems. Psychotic breakdowns, in the class room and elsewhere, are not treated as psychotic breakdowns, but as normal behavior. When professors are the target, they are at fault.

Just as all beliefs are equally valid, so all behavior is equally acceptable. Then the campus in its appeal to reason and rationality (in the form just now portrayed) is unable to say, "You are behaving in an inappropriate way." "This is wrong." "This falls outside the range of correct behavior." Or simply: "No."

That accounts for the failure not only of intellectual standards, but even of rules of routine civility, as out-going President Swearer himself noted in his farewell address to the students. And it explains why, when the students attack the professors, which is commonplace at Brown, the professors are put on trial, not the students.

So in the renewal of higher education, the curriculum demands attention. And that means sustained and serious rethinking of what we think and teach, and why it is worthwhile to think and teach what we do, rather than something else.

Pioneering in the renewal of what was good, leaders in the renovation and in the innovation in higher learning will win for some universities that paramount position in the intellectual life of this country that today is filled by universities lacking all educational purpose. These stand as the relics of a discredited age.

Where are the leaders of learning in the twenty-first century? The country waits for its future Harvards and Yales and Stanfords, which led but now lead no more. Intellectual bankruptcy at the once-prestigious universities represents a great opportunity for a new entrepreneurship, initiatives of the intellect in the free market of ideas.

For the opportunity for greatness tomorrow is contained in today's challenge of regaining for universities access to intellect, which means of rebuilding high ideals of higher education into the life of colleges and universities.

Chapter 5

The Social Contract in the College Classroom

Here, I speak not to trustees, presidents, and professors, but students. And, therefore, I invent the occasion of the beginning of the year, while, for a brief moment, the students focus upon what they are doing in college.

The beginning of the school year challenges us to ask tough questions: what do I expect in the next ten months or so? For, you don't have to be here, and it's costing plenty of money for you to stay here. Not only so, but the more conservative colleges and universities still take teaching seriously, and are not expensive baby-sitting operations. Your families have sent you here, and your college and its professors have received you here, because they, and you, must agree it is the most important thing you can do with your life this year. You should therefore ask why. Given all of the many things you can do with your time and money, why should you turn your back on everything else in the world and spend the next ten months here, in these class rooms and laboratories and library, and with these professors? Only if the answer is "because there is nothing more important" should you stay here. And, why should that be so? Because you're going to learn things here that matter and that you cannot learn in any other place or circumstance. What that means has nothing to do with acquiring information; you can learn more from an encyclopedia than you can from me or any other professor. What it means is that you're going to learn in a way in which you can only learn here and nowhere else: that is the social contract of the college class room; it is what we promise you, and what you must demand of us.

Since everybody knows we learn all the time and everywhere, that is a considerable claim in behalf of the thousands of colleges and universities in this country, public and private, religious and secular, famous and homely, where, this morning, a year of studies starts. Why do I think you've made the right decision to come here? Why is this the most important thing you can do with your life this year, this month, this minute? The answer is because here, if your teachers teach and if you learn, you will learn a new way of learning, one that will guide you for all time to come. That's the one point I want to leave with you: demand of your teachers and yourself not merely information, but a way of learning that you can use every day for the rest of your life. It is what we professors promise, and sometimes even deliver: the secret of how to learn by discovering things on your own, of how to learn not by asking but by finding out on your own.

It is the particularly American way of learning, which is by discovering things for yourself. We American professors at our best, aim at teaching by helping students learn on their own. Our theory of teaching is to tell students, "Don't ask, discover!" The more we tell you, the less you learn. The more you learn, the more we teach. And learning takes place, in a country as practical and as rich in innovation as this country, when you find out for yourself. Professors are there to guide, to help, to goad, to irritate, to stimulate. Students are there to explore, to inquire, to ask questions, to experiment, to negotiate knowledge. The ideal teachers for our students, therefore, are people like Socrates, Jesus, and Hillel; and what you have to ask of your professors here is that they measure themselves by the model of Socrates, Jesus, and Hillel. To understand why, I have to tell you what happened to me when I taught in Germany last spring: it was a catastrophe; no one was less well equipped to teach there than I was because I teach by asking questions—but also by listening to the answers, then asking more questions. I don't know any other way. I think that's the best way, and it's the way of Socrates, Jesus, and Hilel, and a great many professors in this country's colleges and universities: don't ask, discover.

I realized last spring how different is our theory of teaching from that of Europeans when I was a visiting professor at the University of Frankfurt, in Germany, for a semester. For my part, I had a very good time; but for theirs, I think the students didn't. Because, as they put it to me, "All you do is ask us questions. When are you going to tell us what you want us to think?" That was a dreadful moment for me. I've spent my whole life teaching through asking questions and listening to the answers and then asking questions, teaching through a process of negotiation and dialogue; and I am really not equipped to walk into a class room and tell people things. I learned early in my teaching career that when I walked into the class room with a "brilliant" lecture and gave it, I felt wonderful, and the students thought I was a babbler. But, when an older colleague walked in, and, in a very simple way, talked through his subject, asking questions, telling stories, bobbing and weaving as he went, the students not only loved him; they loved what he was saying and made it their own. That was my first lesson in teaching, five years out of graduate school; and I spent the last thirty years as a beginner, still trying to do at all what that colleague did so well, so effortlessly: draw students in, guide them forward, not so much like a cowboy with a herd of cattle as a gallant sergeant weaving up the hill and hoping the troops were following—all the time braving a hail of doubts.

So, when I got to Germany and walked into the class room and laid out a problem for the students to solve, a text meant to serve as a guinea pig for analysis, two cultures met—and neither understood the other. Germans make good students: they take notes and learn lessons. American students at their best make great students: they take risks and draw conclusions. That's why I'll take American students over the ones I taught just now at the University of Frankfurt. And, that explains the reason that American students demand real teachers; German students don't want them. Let me explain.

Great teachers don't teach. They help students learn. Students teach themselves. Three of the all-time greats—Socrates, Jesus, and his Jewish contemporary, the sage, Hillel—share a dislike of heavy-weight speeches. They spoke briefly, painting pictures and telling tales ("parables"), and always raised more questions than they settled.

Socrates was the greatest philosopher of all time, and all he did was walk around the streets and ask people irritating questions. Jesus was certainly the most influential teacher in history, and his longest "lecture"—for instance, the Sermon on the Mount—cannot have filled an hour of class room time or a page in a notebook. And, Hillel's greatest lesson, in answer to someone who told him to teach the entire Torah while standing on one foot—"What is hateful to yourself, don't do to someone else. That's the whole Torah, all the rest is commentary, now go study"—directed people to go off and learn on their own.

The great teacher makes a few simple points. The powerful teacher leaves one or two fundamental truths. And, the memorable teacher makes the point not by telling but by helping the students discover on their own. Learning takes place through discovery, not when you're told something, but when you figure it out for yourself. All a really fine teacher does is make suggestions, point out problems, above all, ask questions, and more questions, and more questions.

This past spring, teaching in Germany, I had a chance to compare my students at the University of South Florida (Tampa, Sarasota) with my students at the Johann Wolfgang Goethe University of Frankfurt. The universities have a lot in common. Both are new, urban, raw, unfinished. Both provide most of whatever higher education there is in their cities and regions. Both attract large numbers of kids who also have jobs, who live at home. The prestige-hungry go off to Gainesville or Tallahassee (not to mention Stanford or Cambridge or New Haven) in this country, Tübingen or Göttingen, in Germany. Tampa and Frankfurt get the masses—and they settle more questions about the future of vast regions—the Suncoast, the State of Hesse-Nassau, respectively—than do Gainesville or Tallahassee or Göttingen or Tubingen. But what a difference!

In Frankfurt, no student ever came to my office to ask me a question. In Tampa, it is routine. Your job is to make it routine here.

In Frankfurt, students do not write papers, do not read in advance of class, do not review work after class. At American colleges it's standard. I know it's standard here.

In Frankfurt, students rarely ask questions in class, rarely argue or propose ideas, rarely participate in the shaping of a proposition. At an American college or university, it happens all the time. In Frankfurt, professors talk, students write things down. In our colleges, some students engage with some professors in a shared inquiry. If going to class is not an adventure for you here, it's your fault: make it so. No college in the country is a better place for a partnership of learning than this one: that's what small liberal arts colleges sell.

In an entire semester at Frankfurt, not one student

asked me to suggest a single reading for the course, not one student prepared in advance of a course meeting, for instance, by glancing at the text I had said we would work on, not one student reviewed after a course meeting, not one student wrote a paper or asked to, not one student came to my office to ask a question on anything, though I worked with my door open and took my seminar students out for supper to get to know them and let them get to know me. It's your job to walk into your professor's office; once you're there, it's the professor's job to make you glad you came: because it is an interesting talk.

American students, in general, do ask questions, do know how to argue, do read, do work on papers, do review after one class and prepare before the next one. So, here I teach real students, using their minds in rigorous ways; there in Germany, I wasted a semester on—and among—intellectual nullities.

Don't German students know more than Americans? Without doubt, they know more about more things. They know languages; we scarcely speak our own. In Germany, all students have studied English for nine years, French for five, and Latin and Greek. German students certainly have been taught more history and literature. But, what they know about the things they have been taught is inert facts. If you ask them a question that requires using, in a strange way, some set of familiar facts, they fall silent. It is hard to teach through questions in a German class room. The one really bad day I had in the class room came when my students really did know the facts, but then could not do anything with what they knew.

Our teaching encourages not only discovery but initiative. Good teaching in our schools leads to risk-taking, good teaching in theirs to note-taking. Successful professors in our system present learning as answers to important questions, successful professors in their system go over familiar facts and pass their opinion on this and that. They tell people things. We want people to make their own discoveries.

So, I don't think Socrates would have found a very warm welcome in a German class room, with all those relentless questions of his. All he did was ask questions; he never really gave any answers, nothing you could memorize and say back on an exam. And, with all due respect, Jesus did not dictate long lectures, so the students could carry home thick notebooks. And Hillel would have lasted about a minute and a half— "now, go study"—indeed! Our kids would have given Socrates a good time, and I think they would have patience for a teacher who just told them stories, like Jesus, or who advised them that everything he could teach he could tell them by standing on one foot, like Hillel. Now, there's real teaching: taking the risk of telling people what you really think, and why you think it, and what difference it makes.

In this country, with its tradition of pragmatism and experiment, we aim at helping students teach themselves, asking them questions to stimulate their own inquiry. We do not indoctrinate; we stimulate. We do not just tell people things; we try to make knowledge important because knowing helps answer urgent questions. The best classes state the problem for students to find the answer.

It's no accident that, in America, many of us teachers demand of our students: don't ask, discover! We have an educational tradition that serves the needs of a society in process, a nation never fully finished, a country in quest, a people of peoples in perpetual search. That is why entire fields of learning are founded here—social science, as we know it now, for instance. That explains why new ideas, new sciences find in this country a ready hearing, a warm welcome.

True, we pay a price for this intellectual restlessness of ours: our kids are better at process than at proposition. They seem to know less; when they need to know, they go and learn. So, they spend more time in the laboratory, work harder at writing their own thoughts, do research on their own. But, then they spend less time learning what we know, work less hard at fully understanding other peoples' thoughts; sometimes do research aimed at re-inventing the wheel. We've made our choices. For an open society, an always-changing economy, a responsible politics of participation and endless negotiation, we need an alert, inventive citizen.

What should you ask of your professors? [1] Don't tell me things, let me find out for myself [2] but, when I need help, give it to me; [3] and, when my work is poor, don't tell me it's good. Many professors would rather be liked than be understood; not a few find it easier to indulge the students than teach them. Don't accept from a professor compliments when they owe you criticism. And, love them when they're tough. Proverbs says, "Rebuke a wise person, and you'll be loved, rebuke a fool and you'll be hated." Show yourselves wise, and you'll get professors who care about what you know.

What should your professors ask of you? [1] Don't ask me to sell you my subject; let me explain it to you. Once you're in the class room, relevance is a settled question: this is what you want to know; now let me teach it. [2] Don't stop work in the middle of the semester. It's easy to start with enthusiasm, and it's easy to end with commitment. But, in the middle of a course, it's hard to sustain your work; the beginning is out of sight, the end and goal and purpose of the course not yet on the horizon. Do your best when the weather looks bleak. [3] Don't sit back and wait to be told things; stay with me and allow the logic of the course to guide us both; join me, think with me. The most remarkable student I've ever taught was a late middle-aged woman who audited a course of mine at the University of South Florida in Sarasota; after five minutes in each class session of three hours, she would say, "Oh, is this what you mean?" And, she would proceed to lay out for me the entire argument that I was beginning to develop. Yes, a remarkable student, but I never walked into class without fearing that I would run out of things to tell people in the first ten minutes. You owe your teachers that moment of trepidation: make them afraid they'll run out of things to tell you. They won't, of course, but you'll make them work and give them life. The challenge is not in disagreeing or agreeing, but in understanding: uncovering the logic and accepting its dictates. That you owe your teachers.

Your imagination is our richest national resource, an open and active mind our most precious intangible treasure. That's what we try to do at our universities and colleges in this country: teach people to teach themselves, which is what life is all about during the coming year, and during all the years of your lives and mine. Have a wonderful year, and let me hear from you.

Chapter 6

The Myth of the Elite National University

No major city in this country concedes that its major hospital is a pest-house, or that its museums display junk, or that its symphony orchestra squeaks. Nor are cities satisfied with inadequate schools. In medicine, the arts and music, politics and government, and primary and secondary education, there is good, but no "best." But we take for granted that in higher education there really is a "best," which can be measured by polling college presidents and deans. That conception yields the fiction of elite national universities as against second-class state and municipal universities at the undergraduate level, and it also defies the facts of American life. When Speaker O'Neill said, "All politics is local," he taught us a lesson that applies also to medicine, the arts, education, industry, and business, as well. For American life is lived at home, in the cities, and the states; we are a nation of regions, a people of localities. We have no Paris or London to set the standard.

When we conceive higher education at the B.A. level to be national, we contradict our character as a nation. In Europe, even with their ministries of culture and their national cultural centers, higher education is local. Providing dormitories and playing fields for large numbers of young people away from home is uncommon. University students ordinarily go to the universities in their own cities for the baccalaureate degree. (Oxford and Cambridge are exceptions, along with Uppsala and Lund, for example. The rule is London or Helsinki or Köln or Bologna: mostly local.) But here, large numbers of students are detached from their homes and communities to form transient cities, which in a given form last for a few years and then fade. American higher education is made up of Brigadoons. Higher education takes place here outside of the context of life: work, home, and family. True, the municipal and state universities attract homebodies. But however accomplished the faculties and however able the students, the excellent regional and state universities have taken second place to what is mentioned—by the supreme mentioners, wherever they may be—on the lists of the national universities, the elite colleges and universities. The state-supported and state-sponsored universities rarely make it among the mentioners, and when Berkeley, Ann Arbor, or Chapel Hill do, it is always with a vague nod to "the great unwashed" or to the great rival of Harvard, which is "Podunk College."

In higher education, "best" means national, whether or not the education is awfully good, whether or not the faculty is genuinely accomplished, whether or not the environment nurtures excellence—or even mental health. Like the Cadillac before they found the Chevy II engines inside, we all know that best is best because we all know it; higher education institutionalizes snobbery. You write up your own press notice, then read it back and believe it—"Look what they're saying about me!" In higher education too the future is going to the universities that serve and build and achieve. And, that means to the universities that nourish and are nurtured by some one place: this town, this region, this state—somewhere in particular. Why do I think so?

If people imagine that higher education can accomplish its goals through elite national institutions—and the rest be damned—they make a quite substantive error. It is that we buy someone else's sizzle rather than our own home-grown beef-steak. The real reason is that the self-styled national universities sever the vital connection between learning and living, between learning and working. The national university removes the young people from home and family and community in the theory that, in formative years, where one has worked and lived and likely is going to work and live no longer serves. Education works when it serves a purpose, meaning when the university is answerable to the community for the here and now of students' lives. When not answerable, when education is separated from learning for work (if not a particular job), and learning for life, education takes on an unreal, a surreal aspect. What do I identify as forces that confuse and detach, that create a kind of personal disorientation for the students? There are two. One is psychological; the other social.

You pay a very heavy emotional price for the sense of having been chosen: you doubt whether you are all that good—and rightly so. The competition to gain entry into the so-called national elite universities is brutal, and for every one who is chosen, ten are rejected. The selection process confers upon the chosen not only pride but also self-doubt. Snobbery and conceit then must cover up uncertainty about one's real worth.

Well, what of the faculties? They too pay an awful psychological price for seeing themselves as the elect. Are the Ivy League professors not the best, acknowledged and marked and certified as more important than the Podunk professors because after all, they have been chosen for their eminent posts? That kind of automatic ranking may save the rest of the world the labor of reading what they write, and even of inquiring into their excellence as teachers. Alas, it is at best unproven and at worst true only part of the time, which means, as a rule of thumb, false most of the time.

Even professors at the elite schools know full well that if we invoke the criterion of national ranking department by department, meaning exactly how good are your professors in their professed subjects, then the labor-saving device of assuming excellence because of position misleads. It is true not only in politics or music or journalism but also in education: it is not the position that honors the person, but the person that honors the position. Every informed person knows that no university today is "best" in all departments or even most of them, and the most prestigious universities turn out to rely for their fame upon their professional schools rather than on their college and graduate faculties. That is why the faculties, no less than the students, at the elect universities pay a heavy price in uncertainty about themselves: do I really belong here? Like acting careers, which most of the time leave the actor or actress unemployed and uncertain, so the professorial careers at the national universities generate considerable unease.

And well they should, since excellence turns out to be distributed not by the university, but by the field. Some fields are so well-conceived and so professionally carried on that nearly everywhere you find excellence, the natural sciences, mathematics, engineering and technology, for example. Some fields are so imprecise and unfocused that people cannot even tell you of what excellence consists, and the result is fields riven with politics and personalities. The aggressive sectarianism of literary criticism, anthropology, and semiotics supplies only the more dreadful examples. When universities excel, it is commonly in the natural sciences and related subjects, and where they are weak, it is in the humanities, with the softer (not quantifiable) social sciences, hotbeds for self-important opinion-mongering, running a close second. And that characterization applies, alas, not only at Podunk College but throughout the elite universities as the deplorable condition of comparative literature at any ten national universities attests for all to see. So excellence turns out to attest to the state of a field of learning rather than to the condition of a given university, another reason for the psychological costs paid by those who find themselves among the chosen few.

No objective facts correlate the national repute of a university and the uniform excellence of its faculty; there is no consistent correlation either between the quality of mind and intellect as expressed in solid achievement in publication and intellectual influence or individual professors and the "name" of the university that employs them. There is a simple rule of thumb: good people are where they are, good work comes from where it comes from; there is today no university press that automatically marks a book as excellent because it comes from that press. Important minds are where they are, and they impart prestige to the colleges or universities where they do their work. Does anybody remember Koenigsburg but that Kant worked there? And who cares whether or not Einstein was a professor in Tübingen or Basel, or Darwin in Cambridge or Leeds, or Freud in Vienna, or Marx in Frankfurt? Greatness is the large-mindedness of the faculty. But if good people are where they are, then greatness can be everywhere.

That brings us back to the main point: the self-doubt generated for faculty and students alike at the national, elite, private, residential universities conflicts with public professions of distinction. When baseball fans parade "We're the best," it's because their team has won the pennant. When students and professors boast, it is with or without high rankings in *U.S. News and World Report*. Inflated endowments, great libraries, tradition, and old buildings can form a facade that conceals a shabby intellectual slum. I do not mean to compare Ivy League universities to Potemkin villages, nor do I say that all emperors are naked. I mean only to ask, "Is it worth the price exacted of those students and professors who live lives of conceit and vacuous self-importance—and insecurity?"

And that brings me back to the other point, the social source of that disorientation of faculties and students alike that characterizes the national or prestige universities. It is that their work takes place out of context. If politics is locative, so too is learning in community. And it is community that endows learning with context and meaning: education for a purpose. I mean not so much (mere) book-writing ("research"), but rather education, for that is why we make universities as instruments of social policy. We build them with public funds or tax-exempt gifts; we look to them for the education of our children, the framing of our future. But the national universities have no context; in an exact sense, they are not locative, but utopian.

When we work as professors in a community, for that community, we draw nourishment from our workplace, just as our community draws strength from us. We shape lives that will be lived where we work, we make an impact upon the mind of the community at hand. We see the results of our labor in the lives of our students. And the community, for its part, needs things from us and values our work on that account: their young people need to learn those skills of intellect, to gain those perspectives of learning—that in our scholarship and teaching that we offer as our stock in trade. So the universities that serve at home will inherit the future for a very simple reason. They are answerable to someone, and it is someone near at hand, who cares, because the work of the university matters in an immediate and real sense: real people learning real things with which to make their lives in the community.

The national universities at the undergraduate level rip people out of the fabric of family and home and community, and the state universities answer to the people of their state and serve to build the home and community and—in the nature of things—also the family near at hand. I think that forms the social reason for the utopian and cosmopolitan character of the elite universities, the claim that education takes place in no place in particular. But that conception of education ignores the social foundations of universities: people send us their children and their money so that we may help them prepare to live good and useful, well-examined lives. These are particular people in a particular place. Culture is not utopian but what we do here and now; all politics is local, and education, including scholarship, accomplishes its goals in a community.

That is not to suggest we have no need for national universities at the BA level. On the contrary, highly specialized universities, such as MIT and Cal Tech, will always find a special place for themselves, but their professionalism and their acknowledged eminence in the few things they claim to do justify that place. In the aggregate, however, education works best when learning relates to living, when learning yields to preparation for work, not a particular job to be sure, but the capacity to work in general, and when what we do in the university years leads from somewhere to somewhere. All politics is local because we live at home; education near at hand is necessary and works best when people care: when universities are answerable to their communities, and when the communities sustain their universities in a reciprocal relationship of nurture.

Chapter 7

Snobs Like That Can't Happen Here

"Different strokes for different folks" in academic language is "We have our own culture" (and bug off). Europeans tell that to Americans when we comment about the odd habits of the natives in their own countries. I remember last year, when I taught at Frankfurt University, commenting in a memo to colleagues that the students don't do any reading or preparing for classes and the professors don't talk to anybody, anyhow. In reply, a colleague on the theological faculty there told me, "Well, we have our own academic culture, and anyhow, now I won't have supper with you." I hadn't known he was planning to; neither had he.

Still, just now I saw a copy of a letter that I would have supposed no circle, however tightly closed, would want to have sent from its midst. Write it if you feel better, but trash it—everybody knows that! This thing came to someone at a research institute who had spent some years in graduate seminar with the writer of the letter, which was an invitation out for supper; he'd written a book on the same problem as her last one and wanted to talk about a problem of common interest. After making fun of his name and saying, anyhow, that she couldn't remember the fellow, she declined the invitation in the following words:

"I probably meant to ask around about you, but forgot. You are probably right to think that I have very

83

little spare time. What I do have, I would rather spend with my neglected friends, than dining with a stranger. You presumably know why you want to have a 'meal date' with me, but what could be my reason?

"There are much less awkward ways of making an acquaintance than challenging her, sight unseen, to a dinner. A whole evening in no company but yours? If you were charming enough to warrant the expenditure of time and energy, some Cambridge hostess would have made the most of you by now. Then, you would be the one with a full dance card."

When I chanced across this gruesome document, I thought, "Well that can't happen here." No American professor could be so self-important, none could leap at the chance to insult a perfectly innocent friend of times past, and none would bother to write up and put in the mail evidence of some gray morning's foul mood. Why bother?

But then I wondered—why not? After all, the academy thrives on hierarchy and lusts after occasions to show who's who. We live by selling prestige; education is our by-product. For instance, a friend of mine who is a highly accomplished neurologist, head of all sorts of medical services in hospitals, told me the one way he knows for sure he's really first rate is that he went to Harvard—forty years ago.

Brown made itself a hot school by grabbing up the discards of the stupid children of the glitzy; the smart ones Harvard takes in, the next go to Yale or Princeton. But to send your kid to college with the kid of someone you've heard of—that's worth the extra $15,000 that Brown charges a year over the local state university. So they make out like bandits with an inexpensive, unaccomplished, trivial faculty. Education is not what it's about when you pay $25,000 a year for what you could get for ten.

Lest my Harvard friend be thought exceptional, a Harvard freshman spent an evening telling me about the famous professors whose lectures she'd attended. When I asked her, "Then what did they teach you?" and "When did you ask them your questions?," she said, "Well at Harvard, that's not how it works. Anyhow, we're the best."

So I suppose Cambridge in England is not the only place where people could write, "If you were charming enough. . . ."

Then again, I thought back to my year in Princeton where, at the Institute for Advanced Study, I met lots of people very pleased with themselves for having an office near Einstein's. When I asked some questions about what they'd done in their fields lately—social science, history—the paltry answers stimulated a little essay, "Why the Franciscans Can't Talk to the Birds." St. Francis could talk to the birds; the Franciscans can't, I said, because you can't institutionalize genius. That won remarkably few friends up there in Princeton. They think you can.

When early on, before I wondered in print whether the emperor might be a bit underdressed, I asked one of the permanent folk for supper with some friends, his reply was, "Well, of course, no—I can't. . . ," followed by some incomprehensible mumbling. I hadn't been made the most of by some Princeton hostess. A friend, an IAS Member in Astrophysics, asked permanent IAS Professor George Kennan for lunch. His secretary replied, "Mr. Kennan doesn't make luncheon appointments with members of the Institute for Advanced Study, but if you see him at lunch, you can sit down at the table." *Bow, bow, ye lower middle classes, bow, bow, ye tradesmen and ye masses.*

Don't get me wrong. Both Cambridges are marvelous places because each has a world class library, and Madame "A whole evening in no company but yours!" wouldn't win any popularity contest in the English Cambridge. Everyone who saw her letter said, "Oh, her." So she's not going to win any elections to office in her precinct, that's clear.

And anyone fortunate enough to spend some time at the Institute for Advanced Study or at Clare Hall, Cambridge, its British counterpart, which does everything right that they do wrong in Princeton, knows that those of us for whom they invent research institutes come to daydream and think up problems to solve—not to get invited by Princeton or Cambridge hostesses. They don't like our suits; we don't like their perfume or their conversation. Ray Monk, the biographer of Wittgenstein, writes about Professor Del in his years at the Institute for Advanced Study, "The Princeton hostesses avoided him." They probably thought they'd ruined his life. Meanwhile, mathematics was reinvented at IAS by their outcast.

The point is that the academic world thrives on snobbery. It glories in its honors, prizes, titles, ribbons, and strange medieval costumes. It thinks its controversies are controversies, conducts bitter disputes over honor, prestige, or policy (who sits in which chair on what afternoon). A college chum of mine, John Updike, told me he doesn't accept honorary degrees—"You just have to sit in the sun for a long afternoon watching other peoples' children get degrees in exchange for a piece of rayon"—but then, he's not a professor. Only in the academy can someone write, "You presumably know why you want to have a 'meal date' with me, but what could be my reason?" In the real world, people don't say things like that to one another. They don't need to. Here in the academy, where the stakes are so low, people sink beneath contempt.

Anyhow, that can't happen here.

Chapter 8

The Coming Crisis in Ethnic Studies

Ethnic studies have run out of steam. Appeals to "our viewpoint" and "our unique insight" no longer persuade. Even those supposedly possessed of a unique insight—whether Jews, women, blacks, Chicanos, Asian- and Pacific-Americans, and the rest—no longer choose to exercise their insight in courses aimed at consciousness-raising and ethnic awareness and affirmation. The transparently political goals of such courses, centers, programs, and departments comprise only one reason. The other is that ethnic studies addressed to a particular group prove boring, repetitious, self-referential. So, representative of the state of ethnic studies in general are black studies courses that, it is reported in the press, decline in enrollment, the numbers of black studies programs and departments diminish, and in all, the ethnic balloon has burst. People blame it on the "yuppie-generation," with its interest not in soul but self. But I blame it on the irrelevance, even to blacks, of black studies as exercises in self-celebration, Jewish studies as a statement of Jews' segregation, women's studies as a discourse in resentment.

The tragedy of black studies has been the segregation of that field, as perceived by whites and blacks alike, not necessarily as intended by professors whether white or black (though black community advocates of black studies bear a heavy burden of guilt for the self-validating definition of the field), so that the profound human experience of blacks in America, the extraordinary record of humanity in Africa, the vast representation of society in stress both there and here—these are represented as "for blacks only." Black studies are too important to be left only to the blacks, and Jewish studies only to the Jews, and Catholic studies (the secular and Protestant academy's neglected stepchild) only to the Catholics, and above all, the intellectually provocative world of women's studies only to women. But that is the effect of special pleading, and overall, ethnic studies stand for "us" against "the other."

That failure of ethnic studies is not to the good of the academy since the blacks, women, Jews, and other distinctive groups in American society do have a rich contribution to make to the academy. Their traditions of learning, literature, their records of a particular sector of the experience of humanity, their fresh perspectives on common issues, their treasure of complex examples to contribute to shared inquiry—these enrich the academy. But when the social and intellectual experience of the new constituencies of the liberal arts takes the form of special pleading and yields self-segregation, no one is interested, and for good reason. The crisis of ethnic studies in the academy exists because the ethnics have ignored the disciplines of the academy and because the academy has conspired in the segregation of the new humanities.

So the issue is clearly drawn—"us" vs. "them," or a shared and public discourse, open to all qualified members of the academic world, upon issues of common intelligibility, discourse vastly enriched by the particular record of a distinctive social group, whether defined by gender or ethnicity. When that record contributes examples for a common inquiry, then the record demands attention. When it forms the wherewithal for private and subjective repetition of self-evident important and valid facts, bearing little consequence for "outsiders," it is not an academic exercise and does not belong in the university.

Just now, Geoffrey Hartman, professor of English at Yale, distinguished literary critic, but mere enthusiast and parvenu in "Jewish studies," interviewed in the *Jerusalem Post*, stated that, since "paganism" has any number of representatives at Yale, so should "Judaism." He was referring to the classics department (!) and to the Jewish studies program, housed in Yale's Department of Religious Studies (even though not a single Jewish studies professor is in the field and discipline of religious studies, or even pretends to be). He further maintained, so it was reported, that every Yale student should be required to study a page of the Talmud. As a Talmud specialist in the field of religious studies, I wonder whatever for. And as a professor in the discipline of religious studies, I never before thought of myself as the counterpart and opposite—whether in advocacy or mere inquiry—to my honorable colleagues in the classics department. We teach about a religion; we work out an analytical program of inquiry. We do not advocate the religion(s) about which we teach. That is the work of chaplains. We are not chaplains there to persuade Jews to "be Jewish"—nor are our colleagues in Greek and Latin expected to go out and kill goats.

Hartman represents the ethnic reading of ethnic studies. As a scholar in the field of literature, he understands teaching as a mode of advocacy, as in literary criticism it assuredly is. But in the field of religious studies, for good and substantial reasons related to the intellectual promise and character of our subject—religion after all is the invention of the academy; the world yields only religions—and also our constituency, teaching in the neutral setting of the university class room cannot constitute a form of advocacy of subject-matter. True, the academic study of religion does contain rich argument of an analytical and propositional character. We in the field of the study of religion teach the description, analysis, and interpretation of religions to whom it may concern, not how or why to be a good Jew, or a good Catholic, to segregated classes of (docile) Jews or Catholics.

But there is considerable reason of hope, because the new humanities are engaged in a bitter battle for the soul of the fields as they live in universities. The case of Jewish or Judaic studies (what you call it makes no difference to me) is suggestive. Jewish and Judaic studies have split into two camps, and they are at war with one another. The one is the ethnic, and they meet in their segregated learned society, the Association for Jewish Studies. At their meetings, anything Jewish goes onto the agenda, mixed together with everything else Jewish. A kind of ghetto-babble resounds, with a great many people treating themselves as expert in a great many subjects they have never studied, because after all, they are Jewish. The other is the academic, and they meet in numerous learned societies, not only in religion and biblical studies, but in sociology, history in all its vast ranges of time, philosophy, Near and Middle Eastern and other area studies, anthropology, literature, and so on and so forth. While there is an academic minority of scholars who teach in seminaries and an ethnic minority of scholars who teach in universities, in the main, the academics are in universities, and the ethnics in the Jewish institutions of higher learning, seminaries, teachers colleges, yeshivas, and the like.

A complete and, I think, final split has now taken place between Jewish and Gentile scholars of Judaic studies in universities and Jewish scholars of Judaic studies (there are no Gentiles to speak of) in institutions under Jewish auspices in the USA and Europe, as well as most Israeli scholars of Judaic studies in the humanistic mode (as distinct from the social scientific). A civil war—fought on uncivil terms, of course—

has broken out. There is no more a single field of Jewish learning, whether called Jewish or Judaic studies. Two separate academies have taken shape, the ethnic and the genuinely academic, and discourse between them is becoming increasingly strained. The one side addresses issues of humanistic learning, engages in no special pleading, and treats the Jewish or the Judaic data as exemplary of broader issues. The other side takes for granted the interest and importance of the Jewish and the Judaic data and regards incremental erudition, whether or not formed for a purpose, as self-evidently interesting.

Professor William Scott Green, University of Rochester, writing in *Midstream* (October 1986, 39), states matters as follows:

> From the perspective of ethnic Jewish studies, materials are deemed interesting because they are Jewish. This school of thought is marked by a fundamentally romantic view of all things it defines as Jewish. Ethnic scholarship tends to be avenging and celebratory. Ethnic education, at whatever level, makes learning into a ritual attachment to the heroic people.
>
> Ethnic intellectual discourse tends to be restricted . . . and directed primarily to those within the ethnic group or those who share its romantic suppositions. In short, ethnic Jewish Studies is a self-validating enterprise, designed to preserve Jewish distinctiveness. Ethnic Jewish scholarship serves a powerful communal purpose and, therefore, is highly charged. It aims to teach the Jews about themselves and, thereby, to create a usable Jewish past, a workable Jewish present, and a viable Jewish future. Within this framework, reasoned intellectual dissent is all too often ignored or censored, or discounted and dismissed, as a form of disloyalty and disrespect.

I am inclined to think that, in the coming decade, Judaic studies will complete the break into two essentially irreconcilable camps with little interchange between them. The size of the two camps is roughly the same in numbers, but the distribution is different. The Jewish ethnic scholars of Judaic studies are concentrated in a few places, the Jewish seminaries, for example, along with the Hebrew teachers colleges, yeshivas, and the like (so far as yeshivas participate in the scholarly world at all), and in the State of Israel and its universities.

The academic scholars of Judaic studies, both Jewish and otherwise, are widely distributed among universities, with from one to ten at any one place, but no sizable number anywhere. They are scattered in a second sense. In their universities, they are not assembled in a single department, but they serve in a variety of disciplines and, therefore, also disciplinary departments (e.g., at Brown—history, religion, literature, language, sociology, political science, and the like). In some places, there may be a program or center or even interdisciplinary department. But it is not the same thing as a yeshiva or a seminary or the Hebrew University of Jerusalem and its confreres, in which dozens of scholars, not differentiated as to discipline, form a unified and large cadre in a single school.

But while widely distributed, the academic and discipline-oriented scholars of Judaic studies are numerous. By definition, they want no journals of "their own," since they propose to address the scholarly universe formed by their particular disciplines. They publish in the *Journal of the American Academy of Religion* or the *American Historical Review*, rather than in the *AJS Review* or the *Hebrew Union College Annual*. They also do not form organizations of Jewish studies, nor do many of them join such organizations. They join the American Academy of Religion, the Society of Biblical Literature, the American Historical Society, and the counterpart societies in literary and other humanistic and social scientific disciplines. In those disciplinary societies, they organize specialist sections in Jewish or Judaic aspects of the prevailing discipline. The academic specialists in Judaic studies, giving disciplinary courses in disciplinary departments and also mounting sophisticated, interdisciplinary majors in Jewish or Judaic studies, form a vital consensus on the basic issues of learning. They view the Jews as exemplary, and they address a broad audience of interested but neutral scholars, in a variety of fields, on a common and shared agenda of inquiry. They do not treat the Jews as self-evidently interesting, and the data do not validate themselves without analysis.

The academic sector of Judaic studies proves as productive as other parts of the humanities and social sciences; debates go forward; theses are presented and tested; much for learning is at stake. Green explains matters in this way:

> Disciplinary Jewish Studies . . . apply to Jewish sources and materials the standardized inquiries, analytical criteria, and . . . skepticisim of university studies in the humanities and social sciences. These disciplines attempt to address common questions to various texts, cultures and societies, and thus, deny special privilege to any of them. They reject, in principle, private, self-validating worlds of experience whose meaning is pertinent and can be transmitted only to initiates. Within a disciplinary framework, the study of discrete Jewish materials is shaped by general questions about human imagination and behavior, questions extrinsic to particular Jewish needs, concerns, and pre-occupations.

The ethnic, or theological, and also the Israeli sector, by contrast, which emphasizes other matters altogether, tends to a certain aridity in both method and result. While—if not very witty—wonderfully erudite, little is at stake in the bitter and violent debates conducted under the ethnic and theological auspices, and in a broad range of subjects, publication is limited. What is more consequential than the absence of publication is the poverty of a scholarly program characteristic of the ethnics, since most of the articles in *Tarbiz* and *Zion*—to take two prominent journals of the ethnics—can and should have been written a century ago, so far as program and problem are concerned. The range of publication limited, the volume spare, the ethnic sector of Jewish or Judaic studies finds little to contribute to common discourse, when work on X's view of Y or on the Jews in Z in the year 1904 has been placed on display.

Proof of the complete break between the two academies may be adduced from the conduct of the ethnics toward the academics. The former condemn without reading, receive with sedulous silence major statements, and violate the accepted norms of academic debate. As Professor William Scott Green comments:

> Strong criticism of others' work is an academic commonplace. It is the principal form of public intellectual engagement—the way scholars transact their business—and is supposed to promote the understanding of ideas, the assessment of theories, and the advancement of knowledge. When criticism degenerates into mere condemnation and overt insult, the dispute is political or personal, not academic and professional. When criticism aims simply to discredit, rather than to discern, the conflicting positions are irreconcilable, perhaps incommensurable.

The mode of criticism of the ethnics is to point to "mistakes," which may or may not be mistakes at all, of which much is made. That is a form of discrediting. To prove plausible, however, lists of mistakes should be joined with lists of non-mistakes. Otherwise, the mistakes may prove—if in fact errors at all, and the great authorities pass their opinion on the basis of remarkable disinterest in facts—adventitious. Reviews that list errors but do not list correct statements are invidious and present mere innuendo; they do not persuade anyone who is not already persuaded.

When again the ethnics invite the other side to conferences and then rescind the invitation on meretricious grounds—or no grounds at all! as was the case with the Israel Historical Society and the Jewish Theological Seminary of America in 1984 and 1985, respectively—then we stand in the presence of not debate, but something else entirely. And the something else, as Green says, has no scholarly or academic interest. That is why the future will witness the fruition of what has already taken place, the complete and final break between two completely unrelated scholarly camps, both working on the same sources and data, the one ethnic, the other academic or, as Green says, disciplinary.

The world of Jewish learning thus has broken in half, with a few strong and segregated centers of the ethnic and many diffused and integrated presences of the disciplinary and academic. The two sides can no longer meet and transact business because there is no business to be done any more, and if truth be told, there probably never was. As Green says,

> There is a surrealism to the entire dispute. Ethnic and disciplinary Jewish Studies operate in incongruous worlds, have incompatible motivations, and address disparate constituencies. The dispute between them is bitter because it is pointless. Not enough is shared between them to allow the possibility of communication, much less persuasion.

I find the development of the two worlds of Judaic studies a perfectly natural outcome of that free academy that welcomes Judaic learning on its terms, alongside that Jewish world that nurtures Judaic learning for its purposes. Both are valid terms and purposes. But the absolute and final division between the one and the other has now to be recognized so that we can get on with the work and see it for what it really is, the rather overstated and overwrought statement with which the ethnic scholars have dismissed their enemy and competition.

What we see is simply the end of a monopoly and the beginning of competition. The academic side has broken the monopoly, which cannot be regained. What can be wrong with that? I see nothing so healthy as the free market place in which ideas compete, as they must compete, and in which people make up their own minds. The disciplinary scholars will learn what the ethnics have to teach when (and that is often) they come up with new facts. They will not be much affected by the imprecations of the ethnics; they will go on with their work, and they already do. As Green says:

> Ethnic Jewish Studies, which serve communal political needs and have communal support, will continue. But disciplinary Jewish Studies have taken firm root in American universities, and they will endure there. No amount of ethnic resentment, hostility, or anger can change that.

Green is surely right. I am not inclined to regret what has happened. On the contrary, I believe it is healthy for the Jewish people to preserve both kinds of learning, since there is a vital role for each, the one for the inner world, the other for the sheltering academy beyond.

And yet—let me say at the end—the civil war does no good for Jewry and wastes energy better spent in constructive projects. I see a real need for both approaches to learning, and each has its task and its place. But on the ethnic side, I see none of a counterpart vision. Just now, at the American Academy of

Religion meeting, a young graduate student in a university doctoral program was accosted by a full professor at the Jewish Theological Seminary who asked where he was studying. When he said, "In such and such a university," the JTSA professor answered, "Oh, and have they emasculated you yet?" The student had the presence of mind to say, "Funny, how much you learn about people from the kind of questions they ask you." So much for the (un)civil war in Jewish studies. That is how it is fought: is that a credit to the Jewish ethnic scholarly world? I think not.

The civil war does no good for the Jewish community or for Judaic or Jewish studies. Each party—the academic in the university, the ethnic in the Jewish-sponsored institution of higher learning—has a valuable contribution to make, and neither can work without the contribution of the other. We of the academy know that fact. But we in the academy can make no compromises in our commitment to the academic disciplines that govern all academic teaching and scholarship. Let me say why. Admitting and presenting any subject on other than academic terms represents a statement by the academy of contempt for that subject. That must not be.

So far as Jewish or Judaic studies are admitted on terms of an-other-than-academic character, it is a statement of anti-Semitism on the part of the academy—an anti-Semitism parallel to the racism for the blacks and the "sexism" vis-a-vis women that treats as personal and private, and therefore a matter of contemptuous disinterest, the human record and experience of Jews, blacks, and women. Equality for Jews with Gentiles, blacks with whites, and women with men, requires the human record and experience of all parties to make its contribution to common discourse. No party is abnormal measured by the norm of the other—and therefore, no (abnormal) party may claim special privilege in a realm of private discourse. The crisis facing ethnic studies will come to resolution when all parties accede to the demands of intellectual equality and radical rationality upon which the academy stands.

Chapter 9

The Bankruptcy of Academic History

I can scarcely overstate the importance for the academic humanities of Hamerow's brilliant account of the state of the field of history. Describing the intellectual framework and institutional structure of one humanistic field, such as Hamerow accomplishes here, provides a model for how other fields are to be set forth. Analyzing the state of the art, specifying strengths and weaknesses, outlining current issues for serious debate—these processes of self-conscious thought provide that perspective that is needed for any individual to find a productive place in the field. And interpreting what is at stake in a humanistic field, the why's and wherefore's of studying this rather than that—that labor of interpretation requires the exercise of taste and judgment that transform learning into wisdom and scholarship into enduring insight. That is why I think everybody should read this remarkable book: Theodore S. Hamerow, *Reflections on History and Historians* (Madison: The University of Wisconsin Press, 1987), 267.

Theodore S. Hamerow, historian at the University of Wisconsin in Madison, with such remarkable wit and acuity accomplishes the description, analysis, and interpretation of the field of history that we in other fields of the academic humanities gain a model and a message for our own thinking about what we do and how and why we do it. Hamerow's program covers both intellectual and political questions, describing the present state of historical learning as profession, not merely hobby; how people become historians; "history as a way of life"; and then, of special interest, "the new history and the old" and "What is the use of history?" He further reports the results of studies of the influence of philanthropic foundations upon historical scholarship and provides an account of the world of nonacademic history. I cannot imagine a more encompassing program of describing and evaluating an academic field, its history, practice, and future, and as I said, the result requires superlatives for comprehensive, balanced, and orderly treatment of fundamental questions of humanistic learning.

Hamerow cannot deal with history in isolation from the humanistic world at large. Our graduate students, for example, come from the same pool of young people; our careers work themselves out in the same academic framework; the issues of one field spill over into the other in the face of challenges common to them both. What is particular to history is a crisis of purpose: "The historical profession in America, after some thirty years of rapid change, growth, and diversification, is today troubled by increasing doubts about its purposes and prospects . . . [historians] stand wondering where the extraordinary boom of the postwar years had led them." The crisis, in part, is practical; young people are not finding positions.

But in more substantial part, it is intellectual: the rise of the social sciences on the scale of academic prestige at the expense of history. Hamerow states matters with his usual clarity: "To our society . . . the methodology of historical scholarship appears inadequate for an understanding of the world in which we live." The new subjects addressed by historians, moreover, such as new regions (Africa, Asia, Latin America), new social and ethnic groups, women's, economic, social, and other kinds of history, have only with great difficulty found for themselves a place in the center of academic-historical discourse. The advance of interest in large-scale social forces, in dealing with vast quantities of data ("cliometrics") moreover by its nature, leaves in a state of acute discomfort the received tradition of historical study as an essentially literary art. The good writers claim not to understand numbers; the good cliometricians do not produce great historical literature, so it is believed.

Not only so, but the state of graduate education gives considerable reason for pause. The length of the doctoral years extends beyond all reason—nine years forming an average!—and the requirements multiply and divide. Employment poses familiar problems. "History as a way of life" in Hamerow's rendition will not present surprises to scholars in religious studies. Relationships between and among scholars, the politics of departments and faculties, the eighth- and quarter-point movements upward and downward on the stock exchange of reputation and career—these hardly present particular problems to history, or even to humanistic learning. If two traits dominate the historical field, they are sloth and envy. Most books are written by only a few people; most first books do not lead to second books; most careers are built, by necessity, upon the shifting sands of politics, because they do not rest on secure foundations of achievement. But these facts of historical study characterize our and, I think, every academic field. When God distributes talent, energy, imagination, the capacity to think large thoughts and take great risks and pursue one's own star of curiosity, it is never evenly and always with a trace of humor, so I think. Nothing in Hamerow's well-documented and elegantly presented account of "becoming a historian" and "history as a way of life" will leave anyone in other humanistic fields gasping in either envy or horror: things are the same everywhere.

The consensus that once told historians what to do and why what they do is worthwhile has crumbled. The field is governed by envy and sloth because it has lost its purpose. On that account, politicians take over. History as an academic field has entered an age of academic obsolescence, while a variety of fields, the academic study of religion foremost among them, from day to day gain renewed vigor and intellectual purpose. Let me explain by a personal reference. As an undergraduate nearly four decades ago, I majored in history, American history, as a matter of fact. After taking the best courses given by my college's best professors, I reached the conclusion that history is a field that is intellectually bankrupt. That is why I turned to the study of religion and, eventually, to the history of religion, which I find, for reasons I shall give in a moment, to be intellectually vigorous and important.

Now, decades later, when I consider the ineffable self-absorption of history departments, which, as in the case of Brown's, refuse even to "cross-list" courses given in historical subjects but not under the auspices of the Department of History; when I contemplate the considerable range of historical fields that now fall outside of the range of "official" historical study, such as religion, women's studies, black studies, Judaic studies, among the new humanities, and nearly the whole range of social sciences that deal with historical topics and periods, among the renewed social sciences of the day, I find that judgment of my youth validated every day. Historians are still debating issues of method that already have come to resolution in a range of academic fields and departments, and they have simply been left behind in the on ward movement of learning. That is why Hamerow's "What is the use of history?" strikes me as a mere rehearsal of the evidence that history, as practiced in departments of history, is intellectually bankrupt, because the urgent questions and the self-evident productive methods of the age are asked and pursued elsewhere on the campus. Retreating to a position of snobbery and disdain carries conviction only for those for whom attitude takes the place of argument, opinion of achievement, and self-satisfaction of the call to journey onward.

Hamerow admits that historians find awkward any "rigorous philosophical examination of their discipline, assuming that its justification is either self-evident or inexplicable." Hamerow points out, "The institutionalization, bureaucratization, and professionalization of knowledge has forced all disciplines to define their scope and technique more rigidly. . . . [but, history] remains far less rigorous or structured than most fields of organized study." So Hamerow further admits, "This deliberate avoidance of theoretical speculation is cheerfully acknowledged by many historians." Hamerow deplores these facts, which he links to the decline in enrollments in history courses. But the issue is not merely that historians will not tell us what they are doing and that it matters. When they do define what they think is at stake in their work, the definitions prove not entirely compelling.

The most common argument is that history "can teach society to make more rational decisions about actions to be taken or policies to be pursued." Historians, as Hamerow represents them, make only a perfunctory case for their subject, while claiming to give good counsel about what lies beyond their subject—a considerable contrast to the humanistic study of religion. Historians have claimed to possess "predictive capability," appealing to constants or repetitions derived from the study of history. But the practical value of historical learning, a position that came to the fore in the eighteenth century with Burke, Jefferson, and Hamilton and then reached fruition in the nineteenth century's claim that historical learning formed the most reliable guide to diplomacy and statecraft, today has lost all credence.

The alternative to scientific methodology and positivistic philosophy is conceived to be literary history: the well-written and engaging classic of exposition of this or that. Here, too, the subject matter gives way to the style: anything well-written, without rhyme or reason as to the choice of topic, serves quite nicely to validate the historical enterprise. In the recent past, politically conservative historians have appealed to history as literature as a mode of historical thought and writing, superior to social science-history, deemed the preserve of politically liberal and left-wing historians. Neither side, in my view, has entirely proved its case. The famous critique of Bury's scientism in historiography by George Macaulay Trevelyan defined the issues, which have precipitated only the repetition, even in the most recent past, of the same unpersuasive arguments on both sides. Fine style is not the monopoly of the Right any more than "culture" is, and the Left does not own the franchise on first-class analytical thinking; the Right-historians, after all, ask the fundamental questions of the theory of society that the Left deems settled by Marx.

None of this is very new. The prominence of the field of history through the nineteenth and into the earlier twentieth centuries proves anomalous. History as a systematic and generalizing science, not merely as a haphazard chronicle of this and that, hardly sinks deep roots into the intellectual life of the West. Voltaire's *Pyrrhonism of History and Fragment on General History* characterized history as laborious and deceitful: "I had to squeeze five hundred pounds of lies in order to extract one ounce of truth." "As for history, it is, after all, only gossip. Even the truest is full of falsehoods, and the only merit it can have is that of style." That judgment of Voltaire sounds suspiciously like the defense of history as literature, against what people call "cliometrics" or "social science-history." Curiously, Hamerow's final defense of history shows what is at stake in the demise of the historical field: "... now it did not really matter whether history was an art or a science, whether it was subject to law or chance, whether it could prognosticate or merely guess. What mattered was that it satisfied a profound emotional, psychological, and social need, regardless of its factual accuracy." Once historians confronted the parlous condition of the learning that they produced, their incapacity ever to know "*wie es eigentlich gewesen,*" they were left with an appeal to—of all things—emotions and psychology and social needs. That extraordinary position denies the very defense that the academy has constructed for itself, for age succeeding age: to know, to understand, to explain, to generalize—that, and not merely to judge from unexamined attitudes, and to make up one's mind without the intervention of thought.

Hamerow's description of the position of Oscar Handlin, with whom, as a matter of fact, I wrote my undergraduate honor's thesis, seems telling to me: "To Handlin the reason for studying historical experiences is essentially the same as the reason for studying galactic patterns or subatomic particles or the topological properties of geometric configurations: because they are there, because they are part of objective reality, and because the human mind has an innate desire to explore and understand that reality." I cannot imagine any theory of the academic humanities that would treat as so trivial and subjective the purpose for the humanities. Hamerow places us in our debt in portraying the intellectual confusion—I think, bankruptcy—of a field generally taken to define the public condition of the humanities in general.

Still, as a specialist in the history of religion, I think things are not so bleak elsewhere. In fact, when someone writes the counterpart to Hamerow's splendid account, "reflections on the study of religion and academic religionists," the book will bear quite different resonance, for it will account for an academic field that exercises full command of intellect in the study of consequential problems of humanity in society. But, then scholars of religion have no doubt about the critical and indicative place of religion in the social condition of humanity, even while scholars of history have lost their once-overweening sense of self and science alike.

Chapter 10

The Emperor's Nudist Colony

(*Profscam: Professors and the Demise of Higher Education* Charles J. Sykes. Washington, D.C.: Regnery Gateway, 1988.)

I wanted to hate this sustained attack on the academy and on professors, which condemns everything for which I have spent my life, but I loved every word. This man is a truth-teller, therefore he is shrill, obnoxious, abusive, aggressive, offensive, and absolutely right on every page. His indictment spells out these academic felonies: "teachers who don't teach, students who don't learn, overcrowded classrooms, lousy instruction, the hyperspecialization of the faculty, and the incoherence and narrowness of the curriculum." But, that does not exhaust the bill of particulars. He works his way through the humanities, which he finds illiterate and purposeless, the social sciences, now transformed by pseudo-math into a fake science, and the natural sciences, devoted to advancing, not learning, but lucre. As judge and jury, I find for the plaintiff: a first rate analysis of a major national calamity, the end of the university as a suitable medium for educating young people.

Sykes deems professors overpaid, underworked, unapproachable, uncommunicative, and unavailable. "They have created a culture in which bad teaching goes unnoticed and unsanctioned and good teaching is penalized." "They have cloaked their scholarship in stupefying, inscrutable jargon. This conceals the fact that much of what passes for research is trivial and inane." "They have twisted the ideals of academic freedom into a system in which they are accountable to no one, while they employ their own rigid methods of thought control to stamp out original thinkers and dissenters."

American universities are "vast factories of junk think. . . ." And on and on—and right, so right! These are not the only items, but they form the well-composed and carefully researched shank of the book.

The indictment may appear scattershot, until you realize that every pellet hits a big fat bird. Lest you think Sykes has written a mere diatribe, a scan of the contents shows otherwise. The book is orderly, systematic, well-researched, and it covers scandal after scandal. It conveys, time and again, a single impression: the academic world affords no place for creative and thoughtful people, but only for conformists. Academic freedom serves only those who believe the right things in the right way. Sykes finds the students victimized by a system that rewards research and penalizes teaching. His program covers the flight from teaching and the crucifixion of teaching on the one side, and the vacuity of the curriculum on the other. He turns to research, covering matters in general with attention to "the weird world of academic journals," then academic license, and concludes with his stunning pictures of the humanities ("the abolition of man"), the social sciences ("the pseudo-scientists"), and the sciences ("beyond the dreams of avarice")

Nevertheless, full of admiration for a sustained and well-crafted piece of serious writing, I find the indictment insufficient. In identifying one culprit, the professorate, Sykes has scarcely assigned the blame as broadly as he ought to have. His indictment may suffice for the professorate (Though even here I think he vastly over estimates the volume of publication, since in my observation, most people publish little or nothing, and he thinks one in ten publishes something). But he seems to me to have forgotten three other fundamental co-conspirators in the demise of higher education in this country.

First, there are the trustees and legislators, the irresponsibles, who govern through indifference in the former case and who fund without asking tough questions in the latter. The state universities maintain somewhat higher standards than private universities across the board. The state-supported scholars rarely appeal to prestige and tradition to justify whatever they do that minute. Many of the private ones always do. The total and well-documented fraud that is education at Harvard could not have taken place in Arkansas, for instance. But even here, the legislature funds, in the end, whatever they are told to fund. Boards of trustees of private institutions restrict themselves to the ritual of choosing a president and then back their choice until they fire him or her.

Second, the guilty include the administrators, the self-serving time-servers and careerists. I think Sykes pays too little attention to the mediocre quality of the generality of presidents, provosts, and deans. His account of a few impressive figures—Arnold Weber's handling of the Foley case at Northwestern comes to mind, contrasting with James Freedman's denial of fair play to the *Dartmouth Review*—obscures the virtually unique standing of the few with intellect and courage. The faceless, purposeless president, worrying in this job about getting the next, far more accurately characterizes the universities today. The reason Sykes misses the abdication of leadership lies in his failure to assess the impact upon academic life of the Viet Nam rebellion in the USA. The great academic presidents of that age were driven off campus, and no one took their place: no one.

Third, and most responsible, the students are willing co-conspirators in the fraud. The generality of students has no academic purpose in the four years they spend in universities. We conduct the world's most expensive baby-sitting operation. Students want not thoughtful, hard criticism of their thinking and writing but praise and fellowship. Seeing the critic of their work as the enemy of their egos, they flock to the easy. Professors who go along get along, and students love them. The generation of the eighties, moreover at least at Brown, proved utterly lacking in the most fundamental social virtues, incapable of respect, indifferent to simple decencies such as honor and civility. I had to threaten a lawsuit for defamation to stop Brown students from signing my name to anti-Semitic letters, for example.

Sykes refers to students' role in destroying universities only casually, speaking of "an unspoken bargain between students and faculty throughout nearly the entire curriculum: Don't ask too much of me and I won't ask too much of you. The bargain works for both undergraduates and professors." True, but understated. Sykes says this in the context of the curriculum. But it is more to the point in the setting of the classroom. Why do I find Sykes' indictment if anything insufficient? My own experience of academe tells me that professors alone are not at fault for the demise of higher education; no one ever wanted things to be other than they now are, except for a few cranks among the professorate, and still fewer students. And students, in general, love things just as they are.

The indictment of the students, above all, is lacking in this marvelous work of criticism, and here a personal reference may be pertinent. In May 1981, I wrote a brief pseudo-speech for the *Brown Daily Herald*, "the commencement address you'll never hear." I wrote in this invented, undeliverable speech:

We, the faculty, take no pride in our educational achievements with you. We have prepared you for a world that does not exist, indeed, that cannot exist. You have spent four years supposing that failure leaves no record. You have learned at Brown that when your work goes poorly, the painless solution is to drop out. But starting now, in the work to which you go, failure marks you. Confronting difficulty by quitting leaves you changed. Outside Brown, quitters are no heroes.

With us, you could argue about why your errors were not errors . . . but tomorrow, in the world to which you go, you had best not defend errors, but learn from them. You will be ill-advised to demand praise for what does not deserve it and to abuse those who do not give it. For four years, we created an altogether forgiving world, in which whatever slight effort you gave was all that was demanded. When you did not keep appointments, we made new ones. When you were late to class, we ignored it. When your work came in beyond the deadline, we pretended not to care.

Worse still, when you were boring, we acted as if you were saying something important. When you were garrulous . . . we listened as if it mattered. When you tossed on our desks writing upon which you had not labored, we read it and even responded, as though you earned a response. When you were dull, we pretended you were smart. When you were predictable and unimaginative and routine, we listened as if to new and wonderful things. When you demanded free lunch, we served it. And all this—why? Despite your fantasies, it was not to be bothered, and the easy way out was pretense: smiles and easy B's. . . .

That is why, on this commencement day, we have nothing in which to take pride. Oh yes, there is one more thing. Try not to act toward your co-workers and bosses as you have acted toward us. I mean, when they do not give you what you want but have not earned, don't abuse them, insult them, or act out with them your parlous relationships with your parents. This, too, we have tolerated. It was, as I said, not to be liked. Few professors actually care whether or not they are liked by peer-paralyzed adolescents, fools so shallow as to imagine professors care, not about education, but about popularity. It was, again, to be rid of you. So go, unlearn the lies we taught you. To life!

The next four months saw this little piece reprinted throughout the world, and, on all manner of mass TV shows, I carried the message that students are involved in a fraud of their own making. It was a message that people are responsible for what they do. I, too, bear responsibility for the fact that, in the aftermath, I was forced out of my department and discipline at Brown, which was religious studies; the academic unit I then worked to found was and still is—and was meant to be—Siberia; when student failures brought meretricious charges against me, my "peers" managed to drag matters out for nearly two years of trials (ending in complete vindication, of course).

In general, my campus career at Brown was over that May. I had a job—a great job, in fact—but no career. But then I was no different from most other professors, who want no careers, only cushy jobs. In my case, I had a life to lead: a life of learning. Few at Brown, or any other school, care much for disciplined scholarship; 90 percent of all academic books come from 10 percent of the professors, and fully two-thirds of all professors have never published a line! Brown was not outstanding, even for its mediocrity. At any rate, my scholarship, of course, went forward. Tenure really does protect that very tiny handful of people who really need it; although overall, Sykes' rejection of tenure seems to me well-argued. I can't say it was a terrible loss to be an academic pariah; to the contrary, I just worked harder in learning and research and published more intellectually ambitious work. But it did leave me sympathetic to books that call into question the self-indulgent privilege, the mindless, costly fraud, the utter waste, that is the world of American higher education.

But this country needs well-educated citizens. Where are they going to come from? If universities are failing, what can replace them (and the enormous investment society has in them), or failing a successor and substitute, who can reform them? For the task of the next generation is not only to repair the enormous injury done by this one, but also to make universities useful again to the society that sustains them and believes in them.

Chapter 11

It's Broke, So Fix It: Some Modest Proposals for Saving the National Endowment for the Arts

A bitter *Kulturkampf* is being waged in this country, and the battlefield of choice has become the future of the National Endowment for the Arts. The same fight can have taken place in Cincinnati, where a sheriff arrested a museum curator, or in Boston, where a public TV station showed explicit pictures of homoerotic activities in the name of public debate on art. But clearly, the debate over NEA, now coming to its climax, is where the opposing armies, each with its generals and its standards, meet.

We have reached an impasse. What has gone wrong in the debate over the NEA? The extremes have crowded out the middle. And the National Endowment for the Arts is meant as a consensusagency. The one side invokes the anguished vision of federal censorship, the other side lists the atrocities arts on tax money, in particular, should not commit. Both are wrong, but for different reasons.

The National Endowment for the Arts is not the Ministry of Culture, nor are its funds an entitlement program for artists. Not getting a grant disappoints the artist but does not censor the art. As to the use of taxpayer funds, the people who favor the exhibition of

115

Mr. Mapplethorpe's photographs with the help of public money also pay taxes.

As to artists denied grants—about one in twenty-five applicants succeeds in our grossly underfunded agency!—there is more private money in the arts today than anyone ever had before. Most of it comes from uncompensated artists themselves, the vast majority of whom work without even the reward of appreciation for their work.

Where can we locate the middle position? The answer is that we have a wall-to-wall consensus, from Senator Helms to Senator Pell, Representative Yates to Representatives Armey, Henry, Gundarson, and Rohrabacker. This is a consensus encompassing nearly the entire political community: [1] yes to the arts, [2] yes to the Endowment, [3] no to censorship, [4] but no to paying taxes to help support what an enormous population in this country finds repulsive.

How about in-house reform? With the best will in the world, the Endowment is the creation of its permanent staff on the one hand, and of the arts community that provides the experts to serve on panels on the other. And that is how it should be. But, then administrative reform will not do the job, because there is a built-in conflict between the arts world, which says, "You give us the money, and we'll tell you what great art is," and the political community, which maintains that tax-money should be spent in ways that most tax payers can support.

So there has to be a list, alas, of what NEA will not fund. What kind of language do we have to write into the reauthorization legislation so that, on account of supporting the arts through the Endowment, which I think a vast majority of both Houses wants to do, no one has to lose his or her seat in the House or in the Senate? Is there a compromise that all sides can live with?

To find the answer, at the last council meeting I

introduced a list made up of everything I could find that anyone wanted to restrict, which we therefore would not fund. . . . I, of course, lost handsomely, two to ten, with one abstention. Then I asked, "Well and good, but what have you to propose?"

And the answer: "We do not fund obscenity."

I replied, "But that's disingenuous. For once, NEA gives money; by definition, the project is 'of artistic interest' within the obscenity rule of Miller vs. California, so there can be no obscenity funded by us, and that, by definition."

If Congress has to make a list of what NEA may not fund, then what list can be long enough to specify all the repulsive actions or thoughts that tax funds may not be used to portray? And how detailed a catalogue of specifications can the Congress compose without itself legislating obscenity? The legislative process works poorly when it attempts to do the job of defining the every day work—the task of the executive in a system such as ours. Micromanaging grants is not the job of Congress; the Arts Endowment has made it the job of Congress, and that is why the Endowment is in trouble. But to this we have come, and in the next few weeks, Congress will have to do, within the chaos of floor debate, what the administration through the Endowment has failed to achieve: find a consensus.

What has happened to short-circuit the political process by destroying the vast and vital center? A small number of conservatives do not favor tax support for the arts in any form. By themselves, they could have done nothing. But their allies are that enormous number of artists who oppose as "censorship" limitations of any kind at all on the use of tax funds for the arts. A large number of artists, whom I also respect and not only because among them is my wife, oppose all limitations on the use of public funds for the arts. Just now, Jonathan Yardley in the *Washington Post* cited an artist who maintains, "You give us the money, and we'll tell you what great art is."

Well for twenty-five years we did give them the money, and they did tell us what great art is, and in some tiny fraction of the cases, the choices have struck the center of public opinion with such horrible force that the Endowment is still reeling and may very well expire–with wretched consequences for the arts in this country. For what has happened, as Congressman Williams told the Council last month, is that the NEA has given art a bad name!

There is no escaping the issues of obscenity, pornography, and offense to religious and racial groups, because when the Endowment, a tax-supported agency within the political process, makes a grant, however small, people wrongly or rightly see government sponsorship implicit in whatever is the artistic outcome. The Endowment creates 240 million art critics. So how are we going to make grants in such a way that the standards of taste and judgment of a very broad community register? The time has come for the vital center to assert itself—the consensus that encompasses the names of Senators Pell and Helms, Representatives Yates, Armey, Henry, Gunderson, Rohrabacker, Regula, and Williams.

Last summer, Senator Pell issued a news release in which he supported re-authorizing the Endowment and opposed restrictions on artists, and he also was explicit in rejecting pornography and obscenity at federal expense. The National Council on the Arts, led by New York state Senator Roy Goodman and Florida State Senator Bob Johnson, unanimously adopted Senator Pell's position in the exact language of his statement. I have had conversations with members of the House of Representatives in which, time and again, these same points came out, as Representative Steve Gunderson expressed them: yes to the arts, no to pornography, and no to censorship. This I take to be the vast, middle position, and it is my position. The real problem is how to get from here to there.

In general, public policy is best served when we legislate in general language, working the public will through agencies, not through the specification of do's and don't's. Anglo-Saxon pragmatism favors practical solutions over theoretical definitions. Congress wants to define policy and create an executive agency to carry out policy; it cannot be expected to conduct an oversight hearing every three days. That explains why, these days, people have rightly focused upon what Congress has to do to accomplish the goals of the Helms-Pell, Armey-Yates consensus.

When Senator Pell created the Endowment in 1965, he had in mind not a federal ministry of culture but a federal foundation, that is, a tritium quid, a mixture of a foundation, like Rockefeller or Ford, and a federal agency. He further wanted the Endowment to serve on the local and state level, nurturing the arts in every constituency, serving arts of a variety of disciplines, responding to taste and judgment diffused across the country. That is why he made a major issue out of the establishment of the arts councils in the states as state agencies.

When therefore I say we are not a ministry of culture, I mean we cannot do and were never meant to do the things that in Europe ministries of culture do. We do not have the funds; we should not have the funds. As a matter of public policy, we also do not censor one kind of art or one medium, nor do we favor some other; we could not do so if we wanted to. Nor did Congress, under Senator Pell's leadership, create an entitlement program for artists. Some may have wanted to, but the consensus was behind a small, select, very well-crafted agency, capable of doing, with great effect, some few things that the federal government could accomplish—and that the private sector in the arts could not. And, that is what the Endowment has been: a federal foundation, with a well-crafted task, a well-defined mission, a federal agency that could (in theory at least) always explain what it was doing, and why what it was doing defined the best possible use, in the public interest, of the scarce tax money made available for the arts.

Have I now wandered far from the starting point—how to sort out the extreme claims on the public interest? You give the money, we'll choose the art, as against a long list of no-nos? Not at all; what I mean to explain is how we may reform this consensus agency, meant to please a great many people by enriching the lives of us all in some few, thoughtfully identified projects. My answer is simple: it is to tinker with the structure, rather than prescribe a long list of do's and don't's. If we can re-frame the organization of the agency in some few, constructive ways, we should be able to get on with the business of sustaining the arts in the public domain in such a way that most people will concur and few people find objectionable what we are doing with their money.

In principle, the answer it seems to me lies in a policy of local, state, and regional participation in a variety of Endowment competitions. I derive the principle from what is at stake, which is the issue of obscenity. The definition of obscenity begins with consideration of community consensus of what is offensive, so let the definition of artistic excellence likewise respond to community consensus on what is beautiful, true, and great art.

Specifically, the larger part of problems emerges, in general, from grants made to individual artists, writers and poets, visual artists, sculptors, and the like. At this time, grants to individual artists are made in a national competition. I propose "regionalization" of most (though not all) grants to individual artists, meaning that the administration of grants to writers and poets, visual artists, solo performers, and the like be located in the regional organizations such as those of the South, New England, the West, and the like. Why the regions? Because they may bring to full expression. the consensus of localities and communities—Atlanta as well as Salt Lake City, Boston as well as Chicago. Why not conduct the competitions through the fifty states and the half dozen special constituencies? Because these form too small a base, both to produce adequate competition and to provide sufficient grants. It will be difficult for North Dakota or Rhode Island to conduct a competition for grants to solo performers or poets, but the Middle Western or New England foundations for the arts can do a fine job. Then North Carolina need not tell New York what to do, nor New York, North Carolina.

A technical consideration seems to me worth your attention—the enormous expense of administering NEA. In my five-and-a-half years on the Council, I have seen the administrative proportion of the agency budget rise from around 9 percent to around 11 percent, and it seems to go up between 0.4 and 0.5 percent a year. It costs us nearly as much to administer a $5,000 choreography grant as a $290,000 orchestra grant: panels cost what they cost, and so do staff salaries. Let us share some of the work load with the regions, where some of the costs—travel and hotel, for example—may prove lower.

Now, you may rightly object that the Seranno grant was a state, not a federal action, a decision made in Winston-Salem by the South Eastern Center for Contemporary Art. And I plead guilty: it was Senator Helms's state's choice, not Senator Moynihan's. It's an imperfect world. All I can recommend is that we follow the model of the obscenity definition and appeal to the states and the regions to choose the poets and writers, the visual artists and the solo performers who in their judgment do work of true excellence.

I appeal, therefore, not to the state of the arts, which some deplore, nor to a rhetoric of free expression, which for some substitutes for argument. I am looking for ways to rebuild the Arts Endowment as a consensus agency that uses its very modest budget for excellent and important programs. To me, that means doing much that we now do, in the way we now do it, but doing some of the things we now do in some different ways: a modest proposal at a moment at which, I think, people have grown somewhat fatigued by appeals, whether to freedom or to morality. If I am wrong, so that there is no consensus that favors the arts and the Endowment, that opposes public funds for pornography and also censorship of the arts, then my modest proposals will prove monumentally irrelevant. But then, I am confident, there also will be no Endowment for the Arts. For in the end, we shall not have entitlement without accountability, not for the Department of Defense and not for the National Endowment for the Arts, to name the largest and the smallest agencies, so unequal in size, but so equal in the weight of public concern that attaches to them.

When President Carter had to appoint a chairman for the National Endowment for the Humanities in 1978-1979, he was reported to have said that he found himself subjected to the heaviest pressures he knew in making any appointment—and he (quite fairly) confessed he was not sure what a humanities is, anyhow. And I am sure that President Bush, by this point, must wonder whether people care more for a dollar of tax money spent on a bottle of urine and a plastic statue of Christ than five billion dollars for a space station that may prove a source of equal exasperation. But that is how things are, so it really is time for the center to assert itself—I mean, the consensus that encompasses the names of Pell and Helms, Yates, Armey, Henry and Gunderson—and it should.

Chapter 12

An Endowment for the Arts, but Not This One

In April 1989, the destruction of the National Endowment for the Arts began. Now the agency is a shell, bones for hyenas to contend over. In the interim, the country has witnessed the implosion of a federal agency. The NEA is over, and I saw its last days. Let me tell you the story.

That month, it all began with a letter I got from the American Family Foundation of Tupelo, Mississippi, complaining to me (among all members of the National Council of the Arts) about a grant made by a beneficiary of a state arts agency, the Southeastern Center for Contemporary Art, in support of a gross offense to the Christian religion. It seems an artist named Seranno had filled a jar with urine and placed in it a plastic statue of Christ on the Cross and called the result art. For that, he got around $20,000 in taxpayer funds from the North Carolina state agency for the arts. Alone among Council members, I replied to Tupelo, saying, "You're right; we goofed; it's not the sort of grant NEA makes or should make, and I personally apologize." Not only did I certainly mean it, but it was, until then, the standard reply to a valid complaint. When William Bennett was chairman of the National Endowment for the Humanities, from time to time he had to say, "We goofed, we're sorry, we'll do better." And that closed off needless controversy.

But the way of wisdom and conciliation was not to be followed. And therein lies the story of how a federal agency made itself a national joke.

It seems that at that moment, the chairmanship of NEA was vacant, Frank Hodsoll having gone on to his just reward at OMB, and a deputy chairman served instead. Like many others on NEA's staff, the deputy chairman had in mind a step onward and upward in the art world, and indeed, a few months later turned up as business manager of the Metropolitan Opera, a position in which he lasted for scarcely a year. The "we goofed, we're sorry" message hardly wins friends in the outer fringes of the art world, and wanting anything but controversy, the NEA's acting chairman obsequiously sent out in all directions generally unintelligible but sympathetic murmurs. But Tupelo got no satisfaction, such as—the American Family Foundation, speaking for millions of rightly-offended faithful Christians, joined by many Jews, atheists, Muslims, Buddhists and unnamed others who object to the defamation of any religion—had coming.

Still, a $20,000 jar of urine, by itself, would not have precipitated twenty-four months of crisis and the ultimate disgrace of the agency. What did was a catastrophe committed quite outside of NEA's control. A year earlier, we had made a grant to the Institute for Contemporary Art at the University of Pennsylvania for a show of photographs by a man named Mapplethorpe. I say we because the council had unanimously voted in favor of the grant. We were told we were voting for a study of lights, shadows, textures, or some such, so why not? And nobody warned us just what was in the light and what was not kept in the shadows at all. (When Senator Helms's staff and I finally got our hands on the actual wording of the recommendation of the staff to the council, we realized no one had warned us of what we were voting on. So, I told the senator's folk I thought their senator would have been

An Endowment for the Arts, but Not This One

just as stupid as Jacob Neusner. They were too courteous to reply). At any rate, *Piss Christ* was the prologue, Mapplethorpe the main event.

Scarcely had *Piss Christ* quieted down when this NEA-funded show was to open within days at the Corcoran in Washington, and the director of the museum, claiming that she was defending the NEA from mysterious enemies, simply cancelled the show.

This was not only stupid, venal, and malicious; it was disingenuous. The man was dead; now his work was to be censored. The art world was rightly outraged and naturally and justifiably saw the cancellation as an act of censorship. But NEA had no role in the decision. By announcing that the censorship had come about because of threats to the NEA, the Corcoran's director implicated us in her action.

But NEA was not well served by her decision; it was, in fact, mortally wounded. We no longer had the opportunity to confess our blunder, apologize, and take shelter for better days. And since the staff had not told the council what it had voted for in Mapplethorpe's grant, the council could not take the heat, as it is supposed to, by saying we knew what we were doing and we uphold our action (as a majority would have said), or we goofed, we're sorry, as I would have said. The staff had slipped it by us. The entire institutional arrangement Congress had created to deal with controversy—a chairman, a council responsible to Congress and the public—had been subverted by the staff and chairman of the agency.

With the Corcoran's precipitate betrayal of artists' trust, the armies were drawn up, the battlefield chosen, and the NEA was right in the middle: censorship verses obscenity, no negotiation, no compromise, no way out.

And that is the impasse that has ever since prevailed.

On the one side, the art world rightly objected to censorship of art.

On the other side, the political community rightly concerned itself with the use of taxpayer funds in a way that accorded with a broad, national consensus.

For the next several months, controversy mounted. Could we not resolve matters? In August 1989, the prevailing consensus was stated with great eloquence by Senator Claiborne Pell, who had created the NEA in 1965: no obscenity, no censorship. Congressional members Williams and Regula, majority and minority leaders in Endowment matters, concurred. Congressman Yates, the Endowment's best friend on the Hill, a man of wit and conscience, went along. So we had our settlement. The Endowment would not fund the yuckie stuff. And the Endowment also would not place itself into the position of having to tell artists what to do or not to do.

But matters were not to prove so simple. For now, in the fall of 1989, onto the field, riding every which way, out of the west, came John Frohnmayer, warbler, lawyer, Bush's 1988 campaign manager in Oregon, a man more confused than confusing, agreeing with the last person he listened to, armed with the President's personal sponsorship, carrying a heavy burden of sentimentality but a light load of wit and wisdom.

Hope died quickly. Anyone who thought that Frohnmayer, politically experienced and well-connected as he was, might be the right man for a difficult political job, entertained the notion for precisely five days. On Monday of his first week in the job, in fall 1989, I got a call from the chairman: "Jack, I'm pulling the such-and-such grant." I said, "John, you could as well say, we goofed, we're sorry." "No, I'm pulling the grant." "Well, John, I'm with you." But then, a few days later, a staff person announced to me, "Jack, John is going to New York to see the exhibit himself." I said, "What ever for?" "Do you want to come too?" "You're joking!" Sure enough, within another day, Frohnmayer came, he saw, and he was conquered. He announced that he was making the grant after all; it really was a beautiful exhibition; he liked it (or rather, "I don't know much about art, but I know what I like, and I like that," would have been more honest). So that was that. John Frohnmayer was just not bright enough to do the job. He lacked political smarts.

But, of course, it wasn't that, not at all. Nothing was settled, except—forever—the chairman's reputation. In his first week in office, he showed that his word was worthless, his judgment worse. He made enemies of his friends, friends of his enemies, embarrassed the presidency that had chosen him, outraged conservative and Republican opinion, and in all taken a federal agency that had enjoyed, on the whole, public recognition and support, and won for it something worse than hatred: the contempt of vast numbers of Americans.

From then to now, the story has repeated itself time and again. The reason is simple. Frohnmayer says everything and its opposite. It depends on who's in the room that minute. On 17 September 1990, he gave a marvelous address at the National Press Club. He told people that, yes, the Endowment belongs to not only the artists but the entire American people; yes, the Endowment should do the things that the federal establishment does well, such as support for institutions, support for overseas display of American art, support for arts in education, and building larger audiences for the arts. Left out? Grants for "the cutting edge" and the "avant garde" (a.k.a. the yuckie stuff), nickels and dimes to pay out-of-work artists to insult the middle brow public, that kind of thing.

The other side would be rid of what it did not want, which was, "restrictive language" (e.g., you may not use federal funds to employ human fetuses in art work, you may not use federal funds to engage in partisan politics). And the conservative side would get rid of what it did not want, which was the use of federal funds to employ human fetuses in art work or to engage in partisan politics. This miracle, worthy of Solomon, would come about simply because federal funds would be directed toward institutions, rather than individuals; so no further abuse of tax funds could take place as had taken place. So some of us thought: "Ah, the wisdom of Washington!"

Fool that I was, I thought that the lessons were learned, so that in its mysterious way, the political process had brought about its own compromise. The inestimable William Safire reached the same conclusion and celebrated it—alas, believing in rationality where there was none. What happened was precisely the opposite. Whatever Frohnmayer said before the 1990 election, afterward, NEA would go on as before, once the agency had survived its re-authorization. According to recent news, enormous grants have gone to some of those very persons who provoked the outrage at the outset. That is to say, while the disposable budget of NEA at the national level has been reduced considerably, the money they still have is used in a manner that is meant to spite and provoke those of us who thought the NEA should focus upon consensus-building projects in which the vast majority of Americans may take pride. Chairman Frohnmayer tells us he will not even carry out the law of Congress, which says that considerations of decency will come into play—even with the limited funds now in hand. The highest priority then is assigned to precisely the kind of programs that earlier created profound offense. The rump-council, meeting with no quorum, concurs.

What I think is at stake is three issues. First, do conservatives and religious people (outside of the left-wing National Council of Churches sectarians) have a right to participate in the shaping of the political consensus? No, we now are hearing, we do not have to be listened to. Second, do the centrists in Congress, including Congressmen Williams and Regula, have the right to legislate public policy through accommodation, negotiation, and compromise? No, we are now told, they can propose, but the NEA administration will dispose. Third, can tax money spent on the arts materially contribute to the general welfare, or will tax funds always end up provoking controversy and outrage? We are told that considerations of the social order will not stand in the way of NEA's use of public funds in any way the insiders damn well please.

Before the 1990 election, I introduced a motion at the council that the NEA not fund a variety of projects found objectionable by various constituencies. I made my list by polling congressional critics of the Endowment; staff members helped in compiling the items (e.g., no funds to projects that use pieces of a human fetus; no funds to projects that propagate views either in favor or against religion or any particular religion). But one clause was close to my heart, since it was copied verbatim from a regulation in effect for years at the National Endowment for the Humanities: no federal funds for projects that served partisan political purposes. This seemed to me innocuous, sure to win a consensus.

It, of course, lost, with three council stalwarts voting in favor, everybody else opposed. The Hatch Act prohibits federal employees from partisan political activities; the NEA pays its clients to do as they wish. The *New York Times*, outraged as it was, published a letter challenging me to name a single great work of art that was not also a political statement. I replied, "Sure, Beethovan's Eighth Symphony." Maybe the letter was too short, they didn't print it. The *New Republic* printed an editorial about "Jacob the Unwise." The publisher, Martin Peretz, apologized to me personally, "I didn't see it before it was printed," and offered to print a reply. Why bother? I had drawn blood.

Two years after the apocalypse, our side has lost the struggle to preserve NEA as an agency in the service of the entire American people. NEA is held captive by a staff that regards with contempt conservatives, Republicans, taxpayers, the middle class, and pretty much everybody outside of its own circle of radical and extreme figures of the avant garde. And why not, since the staff comes from and goes back into the art world with which it identifies, which is the avant garde. It has formed an identity of interest with that world. Frohnmayer made himself the darling of his staff, which saluted him step by step as he was led by them to defy the political consensus that the agency's friends on the Hill had framed.

But what is at stake is not the agency, mortally wounded though it is. True, it is the only cultural agency that received no increase in the FY 1992 proposed budget. True, from a 20 percent set aside for state arts agencies, the NEA has now to give upwards of 30 percent of its appropriate to them, hardly a vote of confidence on the part of the Congress. True, more than 50 percent of its budget now goes to programs that support not artists but only institutions of the arts, many of these marginal to the actual work of creating art in this country. True, from 9 percent of its appropriation, the administrative budget of the agency is now heading toward 12 percent, and at this rate, we shall soon find that we are spending more on getting the money to the arts than on the arts. All of these sad facts mark an agency traduced by its own leadership and staff.

What now is at stake is the good name of the arts. Congressman Williams, a Democrat and a liberal, with Congressman Regula came last summer to the council and warned us, "You are making the arts, not the Endowment for the Arts, into the laughing stock. You are giving the arts a bad name." So much for the National Endowment for the Arts—what an epitaph!

P.S.: Do I think we should maintain a national endowment for the arts? Yes, I do, but not this one.

Chapter 13

Remembering the Artists: The Curse of Grace

When God gives out the gifts of grace, pray that your childrens' share bring a blessing, not a curse. For some of the gifts of grace—special talents, distinctive interests and abilities, even a unique fate in this life—bring a curse, and not a blessing.

Grace we do not earn or merit. God's gift of grace is what makes one person smarter than the next, one more graceful, one more perceptive, one more eloquent. Grace brings distinctions among ordinary people, marking some as extraordinary in some specific way. And in that way, that person has to shape life, lacking all alternatives. God makes us what we must be, giving us no choice. And that way that we cannot choose makes all the difference. So pray for the grace that blesses, not the grace that curses.

What do I mean by a blessing that blesses?

If you are blessed with special strength and agility, you may make your fortune while expressing that distinctive gift that makes you what you are, what you must be. A ballet dancer in the USSR, for example, enjoys grace that brings blessing—a dacha in the country, for instance. One in the USA does not commonly have two homes. An athlete in badminton gets little from the special grace bestowed on him or her; one gifted in tennis or in football makes a great fortune.

We cannot help ourselves. We are creatures in the

131

hands of not an angry but a rather funny God; and save us from the divine sense of humor. The gift always marks us as special, for most people find in themselves no gift at all: there is nothing special that they must be. They lack the grace God bestows. But do not envy the ones who enjoy that grace, for (for some) the grace brings blessing, while for others, grace produces a curse.

Take for example the gift to think abstractly about concrete things—the gift that makes a genius in mathematics and economics, one who can put together figures and economics, into a magnate, a ruler of the world. What a blessing that gift brings!

Then, by contrast, take the gift of special vision, the power of proportion joined to the special eye of the artist. I cannot imagine a greater curse. Many have that gift, few survive it. For if, in the USA, you enjoy the gift of sight and vision, the power to speak of the inner life, not in words but in pictures, chances are you will starve. Or you will abandon your gift for a life of unfulfillment.

Just now, Martha Graham remarked to me, "Dance has the power to express the inner meaning of man without words—as indeed, do all the arts." But pray your children do not discover in dance, in particular, the mystery of their own being: the joy of who they are.

The artists suffer from the curse of grace, not the blessing. Why? They simply cannot make a living. Whether in playwriting, fiction, poetry, visual arts, the success rate in competitions for National Endowment for the Arts funds is well under 5 percent, while the success rate in competitions for National Endowment for the Humanities funds for corresponding grants to individuals is well over 20 percent. So it is (at a rough guess) four times better in America to be good at writing about poetry as a scholar of literature than it is to be good at writing poetry as a poet.

But the problem goes far beyond money. What artists need more than money is recognition. They must see their pictures on walls, hear their music played by orchestras, enjoy, not money in exchange for gesture, vision, voice, and word, but, at least, encounter in the eye and mind of the other. That is why they make the things they make: to share their gifts. Art comes so deeply from within that at some stage, and on some stage, the artist turns outward. Do you hear me? Do you see? Do I speak to you? Does the word, unspoken, but through gesture or the stroke of a brush, reach from deep to deep? The artist cannot know without response. And whence the response? For most, the world out there, when neutral, presents a vast gray silence: no one looks, no one sees or hears or understands—no response. What a gift of grace is it, when the gift to create dance, poetry, music, or stories enjoys no thanks? Braudel once wrote that the unacknowledged gift becomes an insult. How much everyday insult do artists then sustain, whose gifts do not gain acknowledgment—not today, not tomorrow, not ever? What life was there for Van Gogh and Ives, the one who never sold a painting, the other who waited decades to hear his music played out loud by an orchestra? How much an insult do artists receive in consequence of their gifts?

The few whose pictures find their way to the walls of homes or museums enjoy the required response. The many others who live out their lives in solitary stubbornness, loyal to that vision but deprived of all sustenance out of the lives and vision of others, do not. It is a difficult thing to suffer from the grace of art, a very difficult thing.

We professors, scholars whose gifts require us to spend our lives in learning, have a far easier time. Our gifts bring only blessings. We describe, we analyze, we interpret the creations of others. From that we make a fine living, enjoying the sinecure of tenured and well-paid professorships. The world honors our titles and, by the way, ourselves. We enjoy the sustenance and validation of great and powerful institutions that pay us to do what we need and want to do, anyhow. No one treats history as a hobby, no one dismisses the work of a biologist as a private and idiosyncratic exercise, and none treats as strange and remote the effects of the grace to care about the traits of materials in chemistry, or the relationships among persons in sociology, or the workings of human social groups in anthropology. All these subjects require the gifts of grace: the ability to care about these things in particular, the power of mind to investigate these subjects among all others. How fortunate are we who merely study; how unfortunate are they who actually do the thing.

For, as we say in the federal endowments, if you study it, it's humanities; if you do it, it's arts. And blessed is the person whose gift of grace brings the blessing of wanting to examine and analyze, and cursed is the person whose gift of grace brings the curse of wanting actually to do: to risk the self. That we in the humanities do not *do*, and they in the arts do *do*. And that is what marks them as great women and men and us as small: to risk all and nearly always to fail in gaining a world, except the world within.

So they pursue that personal, that private vision all alone, mostly lacking the validation of recognition, not able to make a living from the gifts God gave them, but worse still, not even given the thanks of a society that, one way or the other, gains depth and texture and fresh meaning from their work.

So come doubt, come despair, come isolation, come poverty, come night, come sorrow, come disappointment, they persist, because they can do no other. Thank God to be saved from such a life. But thank God to be given it too. For they do have what the rest of us do not. Creators, they live like God, the creator of us all.

But still, they rely on their inner strength, which though formidable, does not sustain always and everywhere. Whence their strength, the power to endure? They call upon their inner vision, to do what they have to do, because there is no choice. Because that is what God made them and wanted and wants them to be: artists, nothing else.

The average wage of choreographers in the USA, deriving from the genius of choreography, is under $5000—and they are well off. Visual artists make under $700 a year from their art, in the average. And on and on: the poets make, in the average, nothing from their poetry.

Whom God wishes to bless, God blesses in too much abundance, and whom God wishes to curse, God curses that way too: too much vision, too much grace of gesture or of heart or of imagination. That is what I mean when I say we are in the hands of a God of comic gifts. And what it is to be in God's image and after God's likeness, I mean, to be a creator like the Creator, brings rewards that only God can grasp—but also, the artist, who among us is most like God.

And this is for Suzanne Richter Neusner and for Martha Graham, who, near at hand, each in her own way, has taught me these things: to be grateful for the lesser gifts that are mine but also to appreciate the greater gifts that are theirs.

Chapter 14

Talking Peace, Making War: The Paradoxical Record of Religion

Can we who believe in God and affirm our respective religious traditions address the paradox of religion? It is that religions, all of which affirm peace, form in the world a principal source for enmity, social disruption, and political conflict. When we address the simple fact that today, as for long centuries past, religions talk of peace, but in the nature of things, make war, we face the dreadful paradox at hand: talking peace, making war. It goes without saying that enemies of religion make much of that fact. But, we who affirm not only our respective, very particular religions, but also religion, as God's instrument, have also to face the same fact. If in these days we may make of the occasion of a meeting for peace an opportunity to look inward, asking ourselves tough questions about religion, even as we affirm and honor our own and one anothers' religions, then we may meet the challenge. We may do more than rehearse familiar platitudes on how great is peace, how much each of our religious traditions prizes and affirms peace. Then beyond platitude, we can contemplate that paradox that captures the nature of our being religious and of our religions.

Why is it that great religions of the world like

Buddhism and Hinduism in South Asia, Islam in the Middle East, Islam and Judaism in the Near East, Christianity in Europe, both east and west where they exercise power and influence, teach peace, but make war or cause war? I see three principle traits of religion that form of faith a cause of war.

The first is that religion in its social context defines an "us," and that "us" takes shape in contrast with a "them." So religion, by nature, sustains the social order. It identifies within its group those who are alike, and so it sets apart the like from the unlike. In setting forth its case in behalf of the like, it quite naturally marks the other as unlike—with all the heavy burden of dislike that goes with that characterization. The power of religion, therefore, in holding together believers and forming of them a vivid community, also defines the pathos of religion in its insistence on marking this one as like, that one as other.

Second, religion in its psychological context teaches us to differentiate the near at hand and to homogenize the rest. Where there is a caste system, it will establish a minutely detailed hierarchy within the social order, treating as utterly undeserving of hierarchization or even close examination everyone else. So religion focuses our attention upon the like, teaching us how within the framework of the faith there is better and worse, greater or lesser—but then, by its silences, tells us that the other or the outsider simply demands no scrutiny at all. The power of religion in instructing us on how to identify and classify other persons within our group and place ourselves into relationship with them defines the pathos of religion in its dismissal of the other or the outsider. Consequently, in the hierarchy of value and of consequence, the other loses all the humanity that the intense scrutiny of traits imputes to the one scrutinized: the outside does not matter.

Third, religion in its political context proposes

social policy for a homogeneous political order that does not exist. Quite reasonably, religions address not only private life but also public policy, and drawing upon their own rich resources of ethical and moral doctrine, religions formulate proposals for the political community. But the diversity of the social entity that sustains the political process proves disjunctive, and consequently, instead of holding together and sustaining the social order, religions prove disruptive.

The power of religion is its capacity to form community, to define "us," but the pathos is that, in forming community, religion also defines otherness. The power of religion is to teach us to look for God's image and likeness in the face of others, but the pathos is that beyond "the others" whom we know and differentiate lies the outsider, "the other," who is left without distinctive traits. The power of religion is to define worthy goals for the social order, setting forth components of public policy that accord with our vision of humanity "in our image, after our likeness." The pathos of religion is that, whether now or a thousand years ago, religion has proved unable to cope with difference and change: the social order never exhibited so homogeneous a character as to sustain that vision. So our power is our pathos, and where we are strong, we prove fallible and weak.

Some enemies of religion dismiss religion as a relic, a vanishing remnant of a repudiated past. Religion's very capacity to cause and make war proves them wrong; it is an argument that—alas!—is easy to win, wherever we look for evidence of the power of religion in the world today. But the more insidious enemies of religion recognize but deplore religion's remarkable influence in the world order. Their indictment proves considerably more difficult to dismiss, and it reaches into the heart of the matter. For I think, whatever religions think of one another, all religions affirm that religion, in a given formulation, if not in all formulations, is God's gift to us. In the language of the *Sayings of the Founders of Judaism*, for example, beloved is the human being who was created in the image [of God]. It was an act of still greater love that it was made known to him that he was created in the image [of God], as it is said, "For in the image of God he made man" (Gen. 9:6) (*The Sayings of the Founders/Pirqe Abot 3:14*). To generalize, no religious person can imagine that religion is the enemy of the welfare of humanity, and all religious people (speaking, at least, of their own religions in particular) stoutly affirm that religion is God's greatest gift to humanity.

Where then are we to begin the work of demonstrating for all to see the truth of our conviction that religion not only exercises power but forms God's greatest good bestowed upon humanity? In my judgment, it is by starting with ourselves, specifically by trying to learn how to do something we do not now know how to do, which is to carry on the war that we must fight against one another by talking peacefully with one another. If we can succeed in learning how to do that, we shall produce another and a greater paradox: making war in peaceful discourse. For we cannot doubt, in the nature of things, given the claims that religions set forth for themselves—God's will, God's word, for example—religions must conduct an on-going struggle among themselves, and when they fail to do so, they deny their power and their very nature.

Religions define the social order—for their own adherents. That definition includes but, therefore, excludes. Then those who stand outside the social order that a religion sets forth by definition are outsiders—and have to be. Religion differentiates within but homogenizes beyond, and that too is the way of the world, since what is near at hand and subject to our concern will be differentiated, and what is at a distance and unimportant will not. And religions, by their nature, address society at large, insisting that, since their teachings are true, no compromise can be made with difference, no legitimate accommodation can be attempted with diversity. So when we observe how religions speak of peace (for insiders) but call for war (against outsiders), we discern what are, in the end, the innate traits of religions.

Now ours is hardly the first generation of religious women and men to reflect upon the paradox that what we see as God's gift to all humanity can be perceived as God's joke upon us all. On the contrary, every religious system that precipitates reflection upon the world at large—and most do—asks itself how the same God can deliver so many conflicting messages. For most of the history of humanity, that question has proved chronic, but in the West, from the age of the Protestant Reformation and the Catholic Reformation, as well, and in the Near and Middle East even today, the question has become acute. We can no longer dismiss as merely interesting or try to ignore what a world so close to utter destruction must address: the different and conflicting messages that religions hear from one and the same God. The urgency derives not from what secular, atheistic, and anti-religious persons and forces threaten to do to us to discredit us, but from what we, ourselves, may do to the world to destroy the world order beyond repair.

Now, how, over the four hundred years from the Reformations, have we in the Christian West learned to deal with religious difference, with the challenge of one God saying so many contradictory things through many religions? The first response was to appeal to politics: who governed the country decided its religion, and enough said. That response, of course, proved disingenuous; no one believed that the decision of the prince settled questions of religious truth. It was not a compromise but an evasion. The second response was to appeal to religious indifference. Differences among religions discredit them all equally. But that solution to the problem of religious difference, contributed by the Enlightenment, bore no relevance at all to religions themselves, which thrive because no one is indifferent. The third response, that of nineteenth century romanticism married to nationalism, subordinated religion to the nation, identified religion with the nation, to the detriment of religion. Accordingly, a kind of relativism in disguise treated religion as integral to the life of the nation—with the (generally unstated) corollary that other nations will have whatever religions they want, too. When to be a Pole meant to be, by the way, a Roman Catholic, or to be a German meant to be Evangelical (Lutheran), the many people living in Poland who were Ukrainian Orthodox, or Judaic, or Russian Orthodox, or German Lutheran (to give four examples among many) were excluded from the nation that was coming to be born, and worse still, the Roman Catholic religion, for its part, was made an instrument, instead of the ultimate and goal of all of life, such as the faith (like all faiths) saw itself.

The human tragedy of our own century, in which millions of human beings were "exterminated" like insects, in which the Communists in the Soviet Union starved ten million Ukrainians to death, the Germans built factories to manufacture nearly six million dead Jews in the Holocaust, Hindus massacred Muslims, and Muslims, Hindus, and Muslims, other Muslims, not to mention Christians—this most tragic of all centuries has shown us the virtue of toleration. But toleration, too, is an evasion, and that in two ways. First, when we tolerate the other, we evade the truth-claims made by the other, and so we dismiss them. Second, when we tolerate the other, we pretend that the other is so revolting that we can abide him or her only by a superhuman act of (mere) tolerance. So if we found we did not have to tolerate, we would, indeed, eliminate difference.

Toleration or tolerance proves to be a political, not theological, virtue. They serve the social order, to be sure, but solely in its secular aspect. These are scarcely virtues that religions can commend. For insistence upon toleration for the truths of others imposes pretense that truths of others are really true, but we do not honestly think so. And our theological convictions, which shape our intellects, attitudes, and judgments, tell us one thing is right and another thing wrong; this true, that false. So to survive our century, we have had to make a virtue out of what is, at best, a mere necessity.

The result is that we believers, all in one God but all in different things about that one God, really have not yet begun to think about thinking about difference. Let me give a concrete example of the issues that await attention. In Britain today, a debate on religious education in a pluralistic society's public schools underlines how little religions have to contribute to the social order, and how much destruction their failure to date has wrought to the social order. But the same debate underlines how great a flaw in religions themselves opens to public scrutiny in our failure to learn how to make judgments of the other, beyond mere rejection, vilification, or indifference. Can there be religious education in the public schools at all? Christian evangelicals in Britain held there cannot: religious education is to show "the Way, the Truth, and the Life." Muslims opposed the multi-culturalism of the proposed curriculum, for "the ultimate aim of Muslim education lies in the realization of complete submission to God." Secular and agnostic opinion rejected the "multiculturalist" use of religious education "as a vehicle for politicization in the class room." In this context, Mervyn Hiskett, in *The Salisbury Review* (June 1990, 13-16), asks whether religious education really can "promote respect, understanding, and tolerance for those who adhere to different faiths."

Hiskett raises this question, which I think really demands our attention: "The requirement of 'respect, understanding and tolerance for those who adhere to different faiths' begs some questions and adumbrates multiculturalist attitudes. Few would argue against senior pupils understanding Islam, Hinduism, Sikhism, and so on . . . The same applies to respect, provided this is understood to mean simply civilized and courteous behavior, not the sycophantic 'celebratory approach' of the multiculturalists." But Hiskitt goes on, "tolerance is a different matter," and I quote his language without endorsing or rejecting his view:

> Are we expected to tolerate a religion and its adherents that seeks to enforce the death penalty on apostates, or a religion whose fundamentalists advocate the return of slavery on scriptural authority, or the ritual death of widows on their husbands' funeral pyres; or one that continues to permit child marriage and the stoning of women for adultery? Tolerance, as the multiculturalists, with their dogma that world religions are to be judged solely from the standpoint of those who practice, understand, and teach them, all too often means a denial of the right to criticize and disapprove. It shuns theological argument. It fears polemic, lest this should cause offence. It will sacrifice principle for the wholly spurious appearance of harmony. Such teaching must lead, in the end, to the suspension of all moral judgment and, thus, to a relativistic amorality among those taught along such lines.

My point in citing the problem of religious education in Britain (a problem I hope in the near future we in the USA will face as well) is to point to a simple fact. None of the religions that comprise the constituents of the British religious order today has fully thought through doctrines of the other. Each speaks only to its own. All repress, for the sake of peace, what they really think of the other. But every one of them knows with perfect faith that the other is less, diminished by reason of difference. And when all religions join together in a single society—the classroom in the present case—the only conversation that appears possible is the implausible one: a discourse that takes as its premise the reign of relativism. So, the message is "What they think is right for them, and what we think is right for us. And we are going to suppress our judgments of what we really find repulsive in the other." Now, that is not peace between and among religions; it is merely hypocrisy raised to a principle of public policy. And if that is the only way in which so enlightened a state as the British one can address religions, what can we expect of the many societies across the globe that have yet to come to grips with the vast confusion of language and culture and religion that characterizes every nation? In our minds and in our hearts, we religious men and women think about the world as though at least our sector of it were cogent, harmonious, simple, and coherent. But when we walk out into the streets, we meet up with unbelievers as well as believers and, more to the point, believers in things that, in God's name, we deny.

Where to begin? Once we agree that we have no time for platitudes, we have to take seriously the differences that are among us. And that means we have to cross the border into the dangerous territory of addressing religious difference religiously! What I mean is simple. Until now, when religions have addressed the outsider, they have done so within one of two motives. First of all, they have taken the outsider seriously within the labor of working out the full logic of the true faith itself. And every religion has a theory of the outsider—formed, to be sure, entirely within the frame of that religion's logic, its system and structure and sense of order. So the theory of the other, whether tolerant or otherwise, is one that affirms the self. Second, religions have taken the problem of the outsider seriously when they have had to, that is, when forces beyond the faith could not be ignored. It is only rarely in the history of religions that people have explored the resources of their faith to think seriously about the other in terms that outsiders themselves can comprehend and even affirm.

One such example derives from the Roman Catholic Church at Vatican II, when doctrines of Judaism and other religions came forth in full recognition of the faith of other people in other things, and other Christian communions have made equivalently radical efforts to re-think relationships with Judaism. But the Judaeo-Christian relationship is a very special one, and its traits scarcely characterize the relationships (to speak solely *pro domo*) of Judaism with any religion, or of Christianity with any other religion, in the same way. So what we have been given is a model, on the one side, and an example of how the work might be done. But Vatican II, in the nature of things, is only that: an example of what one might do, not a prescription for what we are to do. And the Protestant, Orthodox, and Roman Catholic communions all together with their power to think about the entirety of humanity and the whole of human culture and their commitment to a theory of a global order that is Christian over time have tended to love the other in a rather aggressive way. It has been love with stipulations and conditions. But, at least theirs is a theory that proposes a religious way of thinking about the outsider that the outsider can comprehend. To criticize my own faith, and not to boast, I have to say that Judaism has yet to formulate a theory of the other that [1] affirms the otherness of the other; [2] differentiates among outsiders, and that [3] in theory (and not only in practice) acknowledges the pluralistic character of the world order, not only across the globe, but even within the social structure in which Judaism dominates. And, having confessed the pathos of the Judaism that I affirm, I may be forgiven to say that I discern the same unaccomplished tasks in all other religions equally: the beam is in my eye, but the mote in yours too.

So at stake here is what we are to make of the other and how, beyond the human bonds that link us and make possible our discourse to begin with, we may move toward religious dialogue. The dialogue of which I speak is not with the outsider, but within ourselves—above the outsider. But the dialogue will take place, if it can take place, only when the outsider, hearing what we say among ourselves, can yet recognize the outlines of the humanity in God's image, after God's likeness, that that "other" also claims to realize. This is a difficult task, because we have few models for our work together, and because we have many examples of the failures of earlier generations. What they thought represented progress—toleration, relativism, the now-current "multi-culturalism"—we see as evasion, disingenuousness, or hypocrisy in the name of social harmony. But, for believers, such as all of us are, what choices are there beyond toleration (which we take for granted), relativism (which we can never take seriously at all), and multi-culturalism (which we reject every time we affirm what we believe by an act of prayer, for example, or other religious devotion)?

The American people are tolerant, but religions require something other than that secular virtue. If we do not believe in mere toleration, if we reject the spurious truce of relativism, and if in word and deed we deplore (mere) multi-culturalism as merely useful, then where do we find ourselves? It is, as a matter of fact, where all of us affirm we are: before God, and what we are: God's children. But then what? Children squabble but grow up, sometimes, each fully realized and whole and different, but still to love one another. The paradox of religion can be that we too can attain that shalom, that wholeness, that peace, that is in submission to God, in God's image, and after God's likeness.

Chapter 15

Can Someone Be "Religious in General"?

Arguments in favor of decorating the public square with religious markings of a non-sectarian character—reindeer, but not a creche—"in God we trust," but never in the name of Jesus Christ—and, for the side of Judaism, a Hanukkah cookie, but not a religious rite—appeal to the notion that we can be religious in general. By that idea, people seem to mean that there is such a thing as religiosity without religion, generalized affirmation that there is a God in the world without specific confession of anything about God. And it is important for people to insist that you can be religious without the specific piety of a particular church, synagogue, mosque, or temple, because religion is perceived as individual and not social, personal, or cultural. Consequently, many individuals may share a rather generalized attitude, and they all may respond with a common emotion to a given circumstance. Then religion is perceived as individual, is not divisive, not partisan, not sectarian—and also not very important. The generic religion is always private and individual—what I believe, what you believe—and rarely appeals to what we have in common or makes demands upon us on account of what we do together.

Generic religion evades responsibility. We say that all politics is local. By that we mean the exercise of power matters when it matters in the here and now.

The same is true of religion: if all politics is local, all religion is social. Religion that is purely personal and private makes no difference in the world, and that is why people in a pluralistic society resort to the privatization of religion, insisting that it is whatever you personally make it to be.

Generic religion also contradicts the character of religion. The reason is not only that what is important to us is always particular: it is the town in which we live, the work that we do every day, and, in the case of religion, the family, the church or synagogue, and the social group that embody the particular religion we affirm. The reason is that we can point, in the here and now, to religion only in its particularities, in its expression in the locality of everyday life. True, Protestant Christianity and Reform Judaism lay heavy emphasis upon the individual and God's direct encounter with her or him. Roman Catholic Christianity and Orthodox Judaism lay much greater emphasis upon the corporate community that, in covenant, all together stands before God and is sanctified by God. But Protestant, as much as Orthodox and Roman Catholic Christianity, Reform as much as Orthodox and Conservative Judaism, form churches and communities, insist on shared doctrine, treat religion as something that matters, because it is something that we do together.

But religion is treated as generic and also private, not because people misunderstand the character of religion as corporate and public, always defining the social group. It is precisely because they do understand that religion is social that they wish it were otherwise, because religions—no longer religion—have much difficult thinking about the other, the outsider, and tend to divide their believers apart from the common society. When universities, for example, of Roman Catholic, Protestant, or Judaic foundation wish to "de-sectarianize" themselves, it is to make themselves more acceptable to a broader constituency of students and professors. Last year, for example, Brandeis University made provision for food for non-Jewish students, not only kosher food; and the laicization of many Roman Catholic colleges and universities exemplifies the same movement. But we have to ask ourselves whether these efforts to accommodate pluralism—and to exploit it—by removing the marks of what makes us special and different, really serve the purpose that the Judaic, Roman Catholic, and Protestant foundation of colleges and universities are meant to achieve.

For when we pretend to be "religious in general" but not in particular, we deny what is important about ourselves, which is the families that bring us into being, the communities that draw us together, the things that evoke memory and impart sense to lives that, otherwise, come from nowhere and make no sense. "Religion in general" represents all religions as equally right, but no religion in particular can make such a meretricious concession. If Jesus Christ rose from the dead and is the Messiah of the world, then my Judaism that yet waits for the Messiah is wrong. And if the sacrifice of the Mass mediates God's blood and flesh to the faithful, then the Lutherans (not to mention the Baptists) are terribly wrong. I refer to matters of doctrine. But in things that count, like politics, any claim that religions are all right and therefore do not matter and should not divide us contradicts the dreadful facts of the ten counties of Ulster, in Ireland, where Protestants and Catholics kill each other; the Middle East, where varieties of Muslims kill each other; the land of Israel and Kashmir, where Jews and Muslims, Hindus and Muslims, compete for the same territory; and on and on. Open the newspaper any morning—and then try to persuade yourself that "religion in general" forms an option in interpreting the world we actually face!

But if, as I claim, religion is always and only particular, then how are we going to live, on the campus in particular, with religious diversity, pluralism, difference? The solution that requires us to deny difference also defies the reality of religious faith, but the recognition that religions are always local, always particular, always divisive because of their particularity, hardly helps to answer the question of the here and the now. In the university, in particular, we had better face that question, because here we have the chance in full rationality to meet the problems of society. Outside conditions scarcely permit. Here we can talk in a reasonable way, negotiate difference, explore possibilities, and try out alternatives. We scholars are used to argument and difference, and our stock in trade is to try things out: check out this possibility, explore that alternative. And students on the campus too have a whole life in front of them; here, there are few risks, and if you make a mistake, you can learn from it. Outside of the campus, the stakes are higher, and people are not at all so used to experiments that don't work and theories that prove false, but therefore fructifying.

So here on the campus, we have the opportunity, and also the task, of exploring how to be religious in full confrontation with religious difference. And that I take to be the principal problem facing all religions in the twenty-first century: not secularism, but success. For it is clear the wave of the future is not with materialism or atheism, but with churches, synagogues, mosques, and temples; religion has survived two hundred years of militant secularism, both in politics and in intellectual life. But can the world survive the now-manifest triumph of religion and therefore of religions? Here on the campus, we had better deal with these questions, and there is no better location than a university such as Redlands, which, after all, was founded by American Baptists and was intended to provide a Christian setting for higher education, but like Brandeis and Notre Dame and other schools has tended in the recent past to stress only generic religion (if that). The opportunity facing the Protestant, Judaic, and Roman Catholic colleges and universities is to demonstrate how we can be authentic to our heritage without excluding the other by reason of that difference.

Having defined what I conceive to be the single most urgent question facing religion—coping with difference—and the ideal setting for experimentation with that problem, which is the campus, let me turn to the practical issues that have to be faced. Three questions seem to me to demand attention at the outset.

First, what lies beyond relativism, the notion that everybody is right for somebody, but nobody but me is right for me? Second, if not relativism, then what am I to make of difference? Third, can people learn together, play together, work together, if they cannot pray together? Beyond relativism lies the uncomfortable work of affirming we are right when other people disagree; relativism saved us a lot of work, but that labor-saving device has now proved too costly to maintain. But we in universities are used to difference: we argue with each other all the time, if we stand for anything and are doing something as scholars. If not relativism, then what am I to make of difference? As a scholar, I celebrate difference; it is what makes work interesting. If in writing my books all I did was rehearse what I read in other peoples' books, I would find life very boring. And, the same is so of opinion, and especially opinion and belief about what matters. Religious people have avoided what divides them altogether too long; so the Roman Catholics tell us less about Mary than they would like; and the Jews have tended not to affirm their deepest belief in Israel, the Jewish people, as holy and covenanted; and Protestant Christians have found embarrassing the evangelical, Bible-believing Christians' insistence on the Scriptures' inerrant truth. But public debate on what matters to us opens the gates to honesty, and evasion, in the end, corrodes. Our lives together are not healthier when we deny difference; we only begin to live together when we tell the truth about ourselves.

Then, to the heart of the matter: what is to be done, or as I frame the question, can people learn together, play together, work together, if they cannot pray together? Yes, there are things we can do together, even while we recognize that there are other things we cannot share. I will not eat some of the food you eat, but I can share with you what it means to live a life in which every meal forms the occasion to affirm my life in accord with the Torah. My favorite novelist and co-author, Father Andrew Greeley, will not marry, but he will tell you a great deal about the meaning of love and sacrifice and service through celibacy—so much, in fact, that in dialogue with him, you will appreciate what it means to love a woman in ways you cannot have otherwise imagined. My Protestant colleague, wrestling with the dilemma of works in a Calvinist religion can tell me things about the centrality of grace that, for me, open possibilities I did not know were there.

What we can do together when we cannot pray together—recognizing the particularity of the religious life—is learn together and teach one another about the potentialities, the choices made by people who are not like ourselves. But that seems to me precisely what colleges and universities do best: tell us things we did not know, things we could not even have imagined, so as to open our minds (and also our hearts and souls) to worlds we should otherwise have never known, worlds that change us because we have known them. In the classroom, we study histories that are not ours and overcome the limits of the narrow and provincial repertoire of choices we think we have—in politics and public policy, for instance, and in the organization of society and culture. In literature, we see how language serves to embody imagination beyond our capacity, ourselves, to dream and to say what we have seen. Difference in religion, too, opens ways to make ourselves, in all our particularity, more than we knew we were, to become more than we thought we could be. In the language of Christianity and of Judaism, which see humanity "in our image, after our likeness" and look for God in the face of the human being, difference in religion shows us the many ways in which, quite plausibly, people propose to be "in our image, after our likeness."

We have affirmed relativism, and we have denied difference in quest of a basis for mutual acceptance. The university claims to seek truth, so we can no longer claim that everybody is right about a mass of mutually contradictory and incoherent propositions concerning ultimate questions. The university claims to deal with facts, and we can no longer deny the facts of difference. But if everybody else is wrong and I am right—and that proposition contains the faith that, until now, none has dared to confess, at least, not in public—then, what am I to make of the other? My answer is, that I must not make the other over into my own image and after my own likeness, but I have to learn to see in the other another way to be in God's image and after God's likeness. True, that is an uncomfortable proposition. But it is an honest and a necessary one. And that proposition proves remarkably congruent to what we are here to do together, in this particular place, this university, which is to learn. To affirm difference because from it we learn forms the finest religious response to the questions raised when we recognize that religion, like politics, always is local; we cannot be religious in general, because there is, out there in the world at large, not religion but only religions; and the facts that religions are plural and we are diverse present to universities the challenge to become what they claim to be: places in which we entertain a variety of proposals about various subjects, places in which we are one in dialogue, but multiple in perspective, united in respect for reason, utterly divided on all else. Argument is to be enjoyed, not avoided; difference of opinion explored, not evaded—and all for sound, theological reasons: each of us is, after all, "in our image, after our likeness," showing from God's perspective in Scripture just how things are meant to be. And that is, alas, precisely the way they are.

Chapter 16

Tolerance or Complementarity? How Religions Can Get Along in a Pluralist America

The conception of "shalom," as we all know, involves peace in the sense not merely of the absence of war but the presence of a whole and complete state of complementarity. Peace is peace when both parties affirm peace, meaning when each party affirms the other. That commonplace comes to mind here and now in particular because of the poignant confrontation that takes place between two communities that prize peace and seek harmony, the Roman Catholic order of the Carmelites, and the community of Judaism formed by the survivors of the Holocaust. In the conflict presently working itself out in the matter of the location of a place of prayer and communion, we witness yet further evidence that peace is possible only when a whole and complementary understanding among different religions is attained. There can be no peace, nor even a truce, so long as one side within the framework of its religious convictions can make no sense of the other side within the framework of its religious conviction. And, it is clear that the heartbreaking conflict that presently disfigures the peaceful and cooperative relationships between Judaism and Roman Catholic Christianity, nurtured by so many in all parts of the world, comes about because we do not now know how to grasp the other, how to make sense of that other in our own framework and in our own terms.

Accordingly, at this very moment, we confront an example of the future task of all religious intellectuals, which is to try to think through a religious theory of the other, a theory framed by each religion within its own terms, but suitable for guiding the insider on how to think about the outsider. The single most important problem facing religion for the next hundred years, as for the last, is that single intellectual challenge: how to think through difference, how to account, within one's own faith and framework, for the outsider, indeed, for many outsiders. True, people think that the most important problem confronting religion is secularity or falling away, but it is clear from all studies, religious affiliation remains constant. Not only so, but when we look at the evidence of our own eyes, we find the vital signs of religion attested in the headlines everyday: Christian civil war in Ireland, monotheist civil war in the Middle East, the breakup of the Soviet Empire by reason of religious conflict—these attest to the power of religion. But they also remind us of its pathos, which is the incapacity of religions to form for themselves a useful theory of the other. That, not secularization, defines the critical task facing religions: their excess of success in persuading the believers, so that believers not only love one another but hate everybody else.

The commonplace theory of religious systems concerning the other or the outsider, consigning to incomprehensibility the different and the other, finds ample illustration here. What do you do with the outsider? Find the other crazy (as we did Ayatollah Khomeini and Jim Jones of Jonestown), or declare the other the work of the devil (as the Ayatollah did with us), or declare the other subject to such metaphors as unclean, impure, dangerous, and to be exterminated, as the Germans, Christians and ex-Christians alike, did with the Jews? In the case of the tragedy unfolding at Auschwitz, the theory of the other is difficult to express; I am confident that the Carmelite Sisters have only good will for all persons, and I am equally certain that the Jewish survivors, bearers of the moral heritage of the Jewish people and of Judaism in this setting, bear no ill-will for Christianity. The one side identifies the site in its framework and in its terms, the other in its context, and neither seems to have the capacity to grasp the viewpoint of the other within its own frame of reference. Therein lies a future of not merely intolerance or misunderstanding but of utter incomprehension. And it is that incomprehension of the other, the inability to explain the other to oneself in one's own terms, that transforms religion from a force for peace and reconciliation into a cause of war and intolerance.

Tolerance does not suffice. A theory of the other that concedes the outsider is right for the other but not for me, invokes a meretricious relativism that religious believers cannot really mean. Religions will have to learn how to think about the other, not merely to tolerate the other as an unavoidable inconvenience or an evil that cannot be eliminated. For reasons I shall explain, they face the task of thinking within their own theological framework and religious system about the place, within the structure of the other ,outside of it. And that is something no religion has ever accomplished up to this time.

Religions have spent their best intellectual energies in thinking about themselves, not about the outsider. Why should this be so? The reason is that religions form accounts of a social world, the one formed by the pious; they set forth a world view, define a way of life that realizes that world view, and identify the social entity that constitutes the world explained by the world view and embodied in the way of life: world without end. The this-worldly power of religion derives from its capacity to hold people together and make them see themselves as not a given but a gift: special, distinctive, chosen, saved—whatever. But the very remarkable capacity of religions to define all that is important about a person, a family, or a group also incapacitates religions in a world in which it is clear that difference must be accommodated. For, in explaining the social world within, religions also build walls against the social world without, and, in consequence, religions impose upon the other, the outsider, a definition and a standing that scarcely serve the social order and the public interest.

For theories of "the other" that afford at best toleration, and at worst humiliation and subordination, may have served in an age of an ordered society, but they do not fit a time in which social change forms the sole constant. It is one thing to design a hierarchical society defined by religion when one religion is on top, all others subordinated, as was the case in the Islamic nation(s) from the seventh century, and as was the case in Christian Europe until the rise of the nation-state. A hierarchy based upon religion, with Islam at the apex and Christianity and Judaism as tolerated but, on the whole, well-treated minorities, served so long as all parties accepted their place. So, too, Christian European society before the Reformation had its dual theory of religious difference within the social order: the Christian state, headed by the Pope, Christ's deputy, and the monarch, the secular Christian counterpart. In such an order, Judaism found its place as testimony, Islam was kept at bay across the Pyrenees or Mediterranean and then forced back in the Near East itself, and paganism would be eliminated. But with the shaking of the foundations in the Reformation, for instance, the social order trembled; Christianity in the West became two, then many, and the hierarchical structure tottered. Then, what of the other?

Jews were driven to the East, the more tolerant, pioneering territories of Poland, Lithuania, White Russia, the Ukraine; Islam would then be ignored; and Christians would spend centuries killing other Christians—some theory of the other! Some theory of the social order!

The solution of the seventeenth century was simple: the head of state defines the governing Church. That served where it served. The solution of the eighteenth century was still more simple: tolerate everything, because all religions are equally ridiculous. But no religion accepted either theory of religious difference, and it was with no theory of the other, of religious difference, formed within religious conviction and loyalty, that the West entered its great ages of consolidation and expansion and fruition, then dissolution and civil strife, in the nineteenth and twentieth centuries. The civil war of western, then world, civilization proved no age for thinking about the social order, and the pressing problem of religious accommodation of religious difference hardly gained attention. The reason is that, from 1914 to nearly the present day, it was by no means clear that humanity would survive the civil war fought at such cost and for so long. With a million killed in one battle in 1915, with twenty million Soviet citizens killed in World War II, a prior ten million Soviet citizens killed by their own government in the decade preceding the war, and six million Jews murdered in factories built to manufacture death—with humanity at war with itself, religions could hardly be expected to reconsider long-neglected and scarcely urgent questions.

Yet, it is obvious, religious theories of religious difference, that is, a theory formed within the framework of a religious world view, way of life, and social entity about those beyond that framework, do impose upon us an urgent task now. Part of the reason is the simple fact that we have survived the twentieth century. In 1945, no one knew we would, and many doubted it. But the atomic peace is holding, and while the competition between our own country and the Soviet Union will take other forms, the threat of armed conflict on a global scale diminishes, because the USSR, at this time, cannot mount such a war.

That adventitious fact by itself would hardly precipitate deep thought within religion on the requirements of the social order: how to get along with the outsider. But a more important fact does. It is that, as I said before, the two hundred-year campaign against religion on the part of forces of secularization has simply failed. Faith in God, worship of God, life with God—these testimonies to the vitality of religions and therefore also of religion are measurable: people go to church or synagogue, they observe this rite and that requirement, they make their pilgrimages, and by these quite objective measures of the fact of human action, the vast majority of most of the nations of the world is made up of religious believers of one kind or another. All claims that secularization is the established and one-way process, and the demise of religion forms the wave of the future, have defied the facts of religious power and (alas) worldly glory. Not only is religion strong in its own realm, religious affiliations and commitments define loyalties and concerns in the larger social world of politics and culture. Anyone who doubts it had better try to explain, without religion, the intense opposition to abortion manifested by one-third to nearly half (depending on the framing of the issue) of the voting population of this country—like it or not. In the formation of social groups—where we live, how we choose our friends, whom we marry—religion remains a critical indicator.

And that brings us back to the century rushing toward us, an age of perilous peace, a time in which, for the first time in human history, we have the opportunity of a period of sustained peace—but only if . . .

We can have peace on earth only if we find sources of good will for one another, for in the end, moved by hatred, we may well bring down upon ourselves the roof of the temple that is over us all. Hatred of the other, after all, forms a powerful motive to disregard love of self, and anyone who doubts that fact had better reconsider the history of Germany from July 1944 through May 1945. At that time, when everyone knew the German cause was finished, hatred of the other sufficed to sustain a suicidal war that ended with the absolute ruin of all Germany; more people died in the last nine months of World War II than in the first five years. And all that kept Germany going on the path to its own complete destruction was hatred: drag them all down with us. So much for the power of hatred. There is then no guarantee, despite the pax atomics that protects us now, of a long-term peace. There is good reason to tremble when we consider how hatred, brewed within religious theories of the other as the devil, for example, leads nations to act contrary to all rational interest; the war between Iraq and Iran suffices to prove that point.

So there really is a considerable and urgent task before religions today, the task of addressing a question long thought settled by the various religious systems that now flourish. It is the question of the other. And the question is to be framed in terms that only religions can confront, that is to say, the theological theory of the other. The theological question of the other has been framed in these terms: how as a believing person can I make sense of the outsider? And, for a long time, that had to make do. But now we have to reframe the question: how as a believing person can I make sense of the outsider with, not mere tolerance of difference, but esteem for a faith not my own?

To expand the question, how can I form a theory of the other in such a way that, within my own belief, I can respect the other and accord to the outsider legitimacy within the structure of my own faith?

I say very simply that no Western religious tradition has ever answered those questions. None has tried. The hierarchical theory of religions has served, by which Islam at the apex made room for Christianity and Judaism and eliminated everything else; or Christianity at the apex (always in theory, sometimes in practice) found a cave, a cleft in the rock, for Judaism, kept Islam out of sight, and eliminated everything else. Judaism, for its part, expressed its hierarchical counterpart by assigning to undifferentiated humanity (Islam and Christianity never singled out for special handling) a set of requirements for a minimal definition of a humane and just social order, with holy Israel, God's first love, responsible for everything else. Of you, God wants civility; of us, holiness: a hierarchy with one peak and a vast flat plain, no mountain of ascent in between.

When we take note of how religions in the past and present have thought about the other, we may perceive the full weight of the task that is now incumbent upon us. For, looking backward, all our models tell us what not to do, but we have scarcely a single model to emulate: a Christian theology of the other in terms of the other for faithful Christians; a Judaic theology of the other in terms of the other for believing Jews—these have no precedent in either Christian or Judaic theology. That effort at treating as legitimate and authentic a religion other than our own, and with it, and on its account, treating as worthy of respect because of their religion, religious people different from ourselves, we have never seen this before. But in the past quarter-century, the beginnings of the work have been attempted, so far as I know, solely by Roman Catholic and main stream Protestant theologians.

I assign to the future the task of thinking about a religious theory of the other, because I can find in the past no suitable examples of how that thought might unfold, or what rules of intellect may govern. In the case of Judaism, for example, Judaism thought about Christianity when in the fourth century it was forced to do so. In the case of British Christianity, they thought about Buddhism when in the nineteenth century it found it required a theory to make sense of chaotic facts. In both cases, we see religions thinking about the other solely in terms of themselves.

The case of Judaism tells us when and why a religion must frame a theory of the other. It is when political change of a fundamental character changes the social world that a religious system imposes an urgent question that must be addressed. In the case of Judaism, that change, at once political and religious, came about when in the fourth century Christianity became the religion of the Roman Empire. At that moment, the new faith, long ignored as a petty inconvenience at best, required attention. More to the point, the fundamental allegations of the new faith, all of them challenges to Judaism, demanded response. Christians had long told Israel that Jesus is Christ, so the Messiah has come, and there is no further salvation awaiting Israel, and that they were now bearers of the promises of the Old Testament and in them the Israelite prophets' predictions were realized, and that they were now Israel and Israel was now finished. The political change in government made it necessary for the people of Israel, particularly in the "land of Israel" (Palestine) to respond. In the prior three centuries, they had not had to respond to Christianity.

What they did by way of response was not to form a theory of Christianity within the framework of Judaism but to reform their theory of Judaism, that is to say, of who is Israel and what is its relationship, through the Torah, with God. And to that theory, Christendom was simply beside the point. And within that theory— that religious system defining the holy way of life, world view, and social entity that was Israel—Christianity did not find any explanation at all. Nor has it ever since. But at least, for a brief moment, Judaism thought about Christianity. Forced to do so by political change, that stunning shift in the political circumstance of a religion affected that religion's thought about, among other enduring questions, the outsider, the other, the brother, and the enemy. And, as a matter of fact, in thinking about the other, that same religion reconsidered the enduring and long-settled issues concerning itself as well. The fact that thinking about the other means we have also to rethink the truth about ourselves explains, I think, why we are so reluctant to do so.

So far, I have argued that people talk about the same things when they have to, and that they talk about the same things also because they can. But when they do so, what sort of discourse emerges? One answer to that question derives from Western theories of Buddhism, as shaped by British Christianity in the nineteenth century. When the British encountered Buddhism, now in the imperial age of the nineteenth century, they faced a more formidable task. It was both to make sense and to justify: to make sense of a continuing presence and to justify their own presence within the Buddhist world. Philip C. Almond just now has demonstrated a fact that, so far as I know, none has appreciated before, which is that the very concept of "Buddhism" is an invention of the West. He says, "there was an imaginative creation of Buddhism in the first half of the nineteenth century, and . . . the Western creation of Buddhism progressively enabled certain aspects of Eastern cultures to be defined, delimited, and classified. . . . the reification of the term 'Buddhism' . . . defined the nature and content of this entity" (Almond, 1989, 4).

Almond's point is that, while thinking they were discovering Buddhism, in fact Western scholars were inventing it. For they formed a category of their own choosing, so as to join and homogenize a vast variety of data that, in their own setting, were differentiated and not harmonized. Scholarship on Buddhism then forms a chapter in the Western response to the world made necessary by imperialism. As Western nations conquered foreign lands and took them over, they had to answer two questions: [1] what is this? and [2] why is it mine? The first question demanded making sense of nonsense, that is the unfamiliar, and the second asked an equally nonsensical question: what am I doing here? The way in which the first question was answered differed from the medieval theory of the other. The medieval Christians looked for analogies to make the other familiar. The modern ones simply made the other familiar by remaking it into their own image, after their own likeness. Being scholars, they not only organized, they also selected the data with which they could conveniently cope, which is to say, books they could bring home, publish, and study in their libraries.

Almond proves, in his language,

> Buddhism was reified as a textual object. By the middle of the Victorian period, Buddhism was seen as essentially constituted by its textuality, and it was that Buddhism, thus constructed and thus interpreted, that was the criterion against which its manifestations in the "Orient" were measured, and generally . . . found wanting. A crucial product of this process of the textualization of Buddhism was the emergence of the historical Buddha. By the middle of the Victorian period, the Buddha had emerged from the wings of myth and entered the historical stage. No longer identified with the ancient gods, distinct from the Hindu account of him and his mythical predecessors, the Buddha was a human figure—one to be compared, not with the gods, but with other historical personalities, and one to be interpreted in the light of the Victorian ideal of humanity.

So in a word, in developing a theory of the other, the British invented Buddhism, defined it as a textual object, published the texts, in all, "determined the framework in which Buddhism was imaginatively constructed, not only for themselves, but also, in the final analysis, for the East itself. . . . this was an aspect of the Western creation of two qualitatively different modes of being human, the oriental and the occidental . . . This fundamental mode of organizing the East" provided a "conceptual filter through which acceptable aspects of Buddhism could be endorsed, unacceptable ones rejected."

For what we see is that the British intellectuals solved the problem of the other by making the other over into the self. These certainties, these self-evident truths and obviously valid judgments—all constituted a representation of the other into the self. And that is at its foundations not vastly different from the fourth century Judaic intellectuals' confrontation of the other wholly in terms of the self, and the thirteenth century Christian intellectuals' reading of the other wholly in terms of the self. That is what people do, the difference between the religious fourth and thirteenth century versions and the secular nineteenth century version being only the honesty and innocence of the former times, as against the ineffable snobbery of the moderns. Judaic theology did not like Christianity, but it did not hold it in contempt, and it did not reinvent it; Christian theology did not like Buddhism, but while misinterpreting through miscast analogies, it did not fabricate it; but the British intellectuals of the nineteenth century made up the other in their own image, after their own likeness—and in their own studies, turned into factories for the manufacture of mass-produced others, all of them in the model of the self.

And that brings us back to our own time, which is, after all, not the twentieth, but the twenty-first century. Ours is an intellectual task, for if we cannot in a rational and rigorous way think religiously about the other, then the good works of politics and the ordering of society will not be done. And the dimensions of our task are formidable. For we have seen what does not serve. Tolerance works only in a climate of indifference; when you care, so it seems, you also hate. Toleration works where law prevails, but the limits of the law are set by sovereign power, and the range of difference on the other side of the border stretches to the last horizon. So are we able in wit and imagination, mind and intellect, to form a theory of the other coherent with the entire structure of the world that our religious worldview, way of life, account of the "us" that is the social entity, comprises? The issue of coherence is critical, and that matter of cogency with the whole religious system explains why theological propositions are at stake. Tolerance is a mere social necessity but, we all recognize, simply not a theological virtue. Anyone who doubts should recall the ridicule that met the position, "It does not matter what you believe, as long as you're a good person," not to mention, "It does not matter what you believe, as long as you believe something."

But beyond tolerance, and before theology—that is where we now stand. The history of religion is teaching us about the failures of the past—so closing off paths that lead nowhere. Can religious systems make sense of what lies beyond the system? In my judgment, the answer must be affirmative, because the question comes with urgency.

Where to begin? I think it is with the recognition of the simple fact that the world really is different, beyond its difference from us. By that I mean religious systems differentiate within but homogenize the world beyond. They find it possible to conduct a detailed exegesis of their own social order, forming their own hierarchy within; but when it comes to the world beyond the limits of the system, everything is represented as pretty much the same. And that is a component of the systemic coping with difference: we are differentiated because we matter, the outside is undifferentiated because it is there, difference is trivial. But Catholics hate Protestants, and the hatred has nothing to do with us Jews, and Protestants have contempt for Catholics, leaving us out as well. And we nurture our spite too. So difference is not only within the system, and that means systems must think about more differences than they have now tended to encompass.

When religious systems address the differences among outsiders, they will quite naturally reframe the question of difference in yet another way. They will not only understand that Christians are all Christians only to Jews or Muslims, but that Christians are profoundly divided. They will also understand that difference applies within: the participants of a system participate in many systems. Pluralism is existential, not only social; all of us live in many systems, working our way through many worlds, mostly serial worlds, but, sometimes, synchronous ones. I am not quite sure how any of us holds together the worlds of work and home, vocation and avocation, or the considerable range of loyalties that divide our hearts. But most of us do. Then, in this context, we are not only systemically Judaic, Christian, or Buddhist. We are systemically defined within other frameworks as well. Those of us who are intellectuals live within one framework, with its way of life and world view and social entity; those of us who are politicians live within another, with its way of life, world view, and political class; those of us who are athletes live by yet another schedule and do other things; and so it goes; and that is to speak only of the intersecting systems of the common life. What shall we then say of home and family and its confusion? In all, the happy chaos of our lives belies the neat and orderly hierarchy that religious systems impute to the social world. Whether or not in times past, people lived so neatly ordered I cannot say; but

Tolerance or Complementarity?

today they do not. Religion matters not only because it integrates; it matters because it is one of the sole media of integration left to us. But for all of its power to define who we are and what we want to be and to what "us" we belong, religion, too, forms only one circle, perhaps concentric, with more of the circles of our lives than others, but coexistence with the lives of only a few specialists. For the rest, religious difference is just another difference. Now that is something for theology to think about. And when theology addresses difference within, then, quite naturally, a theory of difference beyond will take shape. But it is, after all, asking much of a theology of Judaism to think about difference within the social world of Judaism. Recognizing that fact—and it is a fact—after all, contradicts the integrating task that the religious system performs, and that theology is meant to explain. This is a time for intellectuals to do their work courageously. The events at Oswiecim have turned a chronic into an acute problem, and it will be a Qiddush Hashem—an act, like the act of martyrdom, that is a sanctification of the name of God—on the part of religious intellectuals, both Judaic and Christian, to meet that challenge as an urgent example of an enduring religious dilemma: making sense of the other in the intellectual tools provided by one's own religion and its theology.

Chapter 17

Are Jews Religious? Explaining the Religiosity of an Ethnic Group

Jews' patterns of religiosity do not conform to those familiar to Protestant and Catholic and Orthodox Christianity. But Jews are an intensely religious community. In fact, they practice not one Judaism alone but two of them. One is a Judaism for the home and synagogue, and that derives from the classic and ancient faith that the world knows well. The other is a Judaism for the secular world, the world of politics and public policy, and that is a distinct religious system, also a Judaism, that the world knows. But quite how the two fit together is not always clear to people.

The received Judaism of the Dual Torah—the oral and the written, handed down by God to our rabbi, Moses, on Mount Sinai—characterizes private and family life. The new Judaism of Holocaust and Redemption dominates public and corporate community life. The Day of Atonement, the Passover Seder, the marriage ceremony, the burial rite, these and other celebrations of the home and family mark the lives of the vast majority of Jewish Americans and Canadians, West Europeans, Brazilians and Argentinians, Australians and South Africans. Engagement with the political issues of Jewish corporate life, typified by work in behalf of Soviet Jewry and concern with the State of

Israel, encompasses the same, vast majority. The concern engages vivid energies, deep emotions. The one set of rites derives, as I shall explain, from the Judaism of the Dual Torah, the other from the Judaism of Holocaust and Redemption. So American and other diaspora Jews not only are deeply religious, but they sustain in their lives of active piety two distinct, if in some ways intertwined, Judaic systems, or Judaisms.

These two Judaisms, each with its symbolic system and appeal to a story of who "we" are and what on that account "we" must do, co-exist side-by-side in the lives of the middle range consensus of Jewry. I speak in particular of Jews who live both integrated and segregated lives: strangers entirely at home in the nations of the West. They want to be Jewish but also something else—indeed, many other things, and so they are. And yet, in the torn but mended hearts of Jews of reform, conservative, middle-range orthodox, reconstructionist, or for that matter humanist commitment, whether those Jews are members or synagogues, or unaffiliated with synagogues, these two Judaisms evoke profound and life-transforming affections, attitudes and emotions. The one serves home and family, the other the corporate community. A simple statement of their ubiquity suffices to prove the powerful influence of the Judaism of the Dual Torah. Nearly all Jews attend Passover Seders, either joining family or forming family for the occasion. When one Jew marries another Jew, it is virtually unheard of for them to have a civil, not a Judaic, religious marriage. That rite too derives from the Judaism of the Dual Torah. The indicator for the other Judaism, the Judaism of Holocaust and Redemption, proves equally one-sided: deep concern for the State of Israel and profound response to the tale of the destruction of European Jewry from 1933 to 1945. When we discern their power and influence and understand how they work, we shall see how and why Jewish Americans and Canadians, West Europeans,

Are Jews Religious?

Brazilians and Argentinians, Australians and South Africans, in varying ways to be sure, constitute a singular people on earth.

In answering the question of whether or not American Jews are religious, I obviously do not invoke as my sole criterion of religiosity orthodoxy in its essentially segregated expression (so familiar in Brooklyn). Indeed, I do not even deal with that small segment of the Jewish American world that finds its way to the synagogue twice a day, that studies the Torah morning and night, that lives out its life wholly within the Judaism of the Dual Torah and entirely within the circles of the faithful. That sector of Jewry, self-segregated and rightly self-assured, raises no questions about religiosity, and it, of course, is religious. It indeed is pious in the profound and rich sense of the Judaism of the Dual Torah. Synagogues of that sector of Jewry, mostly orthodox, are crowded on weekdays and require two, three, or more worship services on Sabbaths. Nor do those Jews (in the main) remain aloof from the appeal of Holocaust and Redemption. For those Jews, Judaism encompasses the whole of life and commitment, however, and both the private and the familial and also the civic and the public life of Jewry join in a single entity, defined within the Torah in two parts. The bulk of Jewish Americans, even here in Brooklyn—not to mention Canadians, West Europeans, Latin Americans, South Africans, and Australians—do not live within the disciplines of the Torah and do not live entirely segregated lives. While in North America, most of those non-observant (in the orthodox sense) also do not affiliate with the orthodox community; in Western Europe and the European communities of South Africa and Australia, they do; but the picture does not change. Jews integrated into the values and civilization of the West have produced a twin-Judaism, the one for the home, the other for the Judaic polity and the life of public discourse, and it is that dual—family and civic—Judaism that shapes and defines the lives of nearly all Jews of the West, those who are not fully observant in the orthodox definition of observance. No study has suggested that the observant Orthodox encompass by any consequential indicator so much as 10 percent of the Jews of North America, surveyed en masse, though in a few major cities, such as New York City or London, the percentage is perhaps double.

In maintaining that American Jews are profoundly religious because they respond to the enchantment of Judaism(s) and are transformed by the wonder of the two distinct systems at hand, I make three propositions in succession.

The first is that words have power. Rightly spoken with proper intentionality, coming from the heart, words bring forth worlds, through enchantment turning the everyday into something remarkable. That is, through the enchantment of its rite, Judaism changes us Jews from what we were into something else, something more, something other than our ordinary selves. The enchantment takes place in heart and soul and mind, comes to expression in deed turned into gesture. A commonplace deed may be to light a candle. A gesture is to kindle a flame to inaugurate the Sabbath. A deed is to eat a cracker. A gesture is to raise a piece of unleavened bread—a cracker of a certain kind—and to announce that it is the bread that our ancestors ate when they hastily left Egypt—and then to eat the cracker. Enchantment reaches fulfillment in the transformation of the here and now of the everyday into the then and there of life with the living God. Enchantment engages the given of our lives and transforms that into a gift.

But second, not all words work. Only some words of Judaism so work as to make worlds of meaning, and that takes place only in a very particular circumstance. That is, in the Judaism that thrives in America and

Canada, Western Europe and Latin America, South Africa and Australia, when words speak to the individual and to the family. Lacking the experience of religion lived in corporate community, people find it difficult to enter into, let alone transform, those social worlds of Judaism that transcend the private life. People appeal, when at home, to one set of rites and their accompanying myths—stories explaining the truth, and they respond, when in community, to another set of rites and myths, telling a different story altogether. The private life and home are changed by rite into holy places. The shared life of the community, lived with other Jews, is not commonly changed by words derived from the same origin. But the life of the corporate community, too, is transformed into heightened being, made to refer to experience and value not materially present. When worlds speak of me, my life, and my family, they transform; when they speak of us, all Israel, all together, in the language of the holy, the same words fall away unheard. But other words, not deriving from the Dual Torah, written and oral, that constitutes God's revelation to Israel, the Jewish people, invoke, evoke, provoke, and transform. Those other words do change us, as profoundly and as completely, as do the words of the rites of the Dual Torah. The same tears come, but the music is different.

And third, another set of words do work for those same Jews, words that make a different world from the one formed of imaginary Israel in the family of Abraham, Isaac, and Jacob. Those other words form a separate Judaism from the one evoked for individual and family on those rites of passage nearly universally observed. The corporate community, unchanged by the words of one Judaism, comes into being through the power of the words of a different Judaism. I identify that other Judaism and explain why, in the context of the religious life of Jewries throughout the free world, where Jews are free to practice any Judaism of their choice, or none, the nature of religion, in general, leads to the formation of the two Judaisms that today flourish, one for the private life of home and family, the other for the political life of the community and its public policy. So I claim to explain why this, not that, in the life of one of today's genuinely vital religions, Judaism in North America and Latin America, Western Europe, South Africa and Australia.

The social world of the synagogue, the concrete realm of worship, presents a different picture from the widespread, popular observance of rites of home and family. The power of theological expression contained within synagogue worship proves deeply affecting on some occasions—for example, the New Year and Day of Atonement, which address the life of the individual, but important on others, Sabbaths and weekdays. The Judaism for individual, home, and family brings Jews to synagogues on some days, not on others, and that explains why that power of liturgy that the synagogue possesses exercises so little charm for Jews that the synagogues stand empty most of the year. The synagogues turn words into a world of meaning specifically on those occasions on which the words address the self. Bare, empty, silent, the synagogues (except only those of a sector of orthodoxy, the self-segregated one living out life only among other Jews) work no wonders when, from day to day and on Sabbaths and festivals, they speak to the "us" of all Israel as a corporate community. "Israel," as the holy society that God has loved, listens to different words from those of the synagogue, responding to a different Judaism from the Judaism of the synagogue liturgy.

Since two Judaisms flourish in the vast middle-range of the socially-integrated Jewries of the West, one for home and family, one for the shared life of the corporate community, we have now to describe each one. The first of the two Judaisms flourishes in the synagogue, as I said, and the second, in the streets. The one is private, the other public, the one personal and familial, the other civic and communal.

The Judaism found compelling in the private life derives from the Judaism of the Dual Torah, oral and written, that took shape in late antiquity—the first seven centuries of the Common Era—and reached its definitive statement in the Talmud of Babylonia. That Judaism not only flourished as the normative and paramount system into the nineteenth century, but now on the eve of the twenty-first continues to impart shape and structure to the on-going life of the synagogue, its liturgy, its holy days and festivals, its theology, its way of life and worldview. This Judaism is familiar from the life of the synagogue and requires no systematic description.

The second Judaism came on the seen only in the aftermath of World War II and the rise of the State of Israel. I call it the "Judaism of Holocaust and Redemption" because it is a Judaic system that invokes, as its generative worldview, the catastrophe of the destruction by Germany of most of the Jews of Europe between 1933 and 1945, and the creation, three years afterward, of the State of Israel. This Judaism is peculiar to the Jewish community and does require a brief description.

This Judaism has its way of life, its religious duties, its public celebrations. It is communal, stressing public policy and practical action. It involves political issues—for example, policy toward the State of Israel, government assistance in helping Soviet Jews gain freedom, and, in the homelands of the Jewish Americans, Canadians, Britons, or French, matters of local politics as well. Let me spell out the worldview and way of life of that other Judaism, one with power to transform civic and public affairs in Jewry as much as the Judaism of the Dual Torah enchants and changes the personal and familial ones. In politics, history, and in society, Jews in North America respond to the Judaism of the Holocaust and Redemption in such a way as to imagine they are someone else, living somewhere else, at another time and circumstance. That vision transforms families into an Israel, a community. The somewhere else is Poland in 1944 and also the earthly Jerusalem in 1967 or now (so long as we are not there, except for a week in a luxury hotel), and the vision turns them from reasonably secure citizens of America or Canada into insecure refugees finding hope and life in the land, and State, of Israel. Public events commemorate, so that "we" were there in "Auschwitz," which stands for all of the centers for the murder of Jews, and "we" share too in the everyday life of that faraway place in which we do not live, but should—the State of Israel. That transformation of time and place, no less than the recasting accomplished by the Passover Seder or the rite of *berit milah* or the *huppah*, turns people into something other than what they are in the here and now.

The issues of this public Judaism, the civil religion of North American Jewry (and not theirs alone), are perceived to be political. But the power of that Judaism to turn things into something other than what they seem, to teach lessons that change the everyday into the remarkable—that power works no less wonderfully than does the power of the other Judaism to make me Adam or one of the Israel that crossed the Red Sea. The lessons of the two Judaisms, of course, are not the same. The Judaism of the Dual Torah teaches about the sanctification of the everyday in the road toward the salvation of the holy people. The Judaism of Holocaust and Redemption tells me that the everyday, the here and the now of home and family, ends not in a new Eden but in a cloud of gas, that salvation lies today, if I will it, but not here and not now. And it teaches me not only not to trouble to sanctify but also not even to trust the present circumstance.

The Judaism of Holocaust and Redemption supplies the words that make another world of this one. Those words, moreover, change the assembly of like-minded individuals into occasions for the celebration of the group and the commemoration of its shared memories. Not only so, but events defined, meetings called, moments identified as distinctive and holy by that Judaism of Holocaust and Redemption mark the public calendar and draw people from home and family to collectivity and community—those events and, except for specified reasons, not the occasions of the sacred calendar of the synagogue—that is—the life of Israel as defined by the Torah. Just as in the USA, religions address the realm of individuals and families, but a civil religion—Thanksgiving, the Fourth of July, the rites of politics—defines public discourse on matters of value and ultimate concern; so, the Judaism of the Dual Torah forms the counterpart to Christianity, and the Judaism of Holocaust and Redemption, as I said, constitutes Jewry's civil religion.

The power of the Judaism of the Holocaust and Redemption to frame Jews' public policy—for many to the exclusion of the Judaism of the Dual Torah—may be shown very simply. The Holocaust formed the question, Redemption in the form of the creation of the State of Israel, the answer, for all universally appealing Jewish public activity and discourse. Synagogues, except for specified occasions, appeal to a few, but activities that express the competing Judaism appeal to nearly everybody. That is to say, nearly all American Jews identify with the State of Israel and regard its welfare as not only a secular good, but a metaphysical necessity—the other chapter of the Holocaust. Nearly all American Jews both support the State of Israel and also regard their own "being Jewish" as inextricably bound up with the meaning they impute to the Jewish state.

That is not to suggest American Judaism constitutes a version of Zionism. Zionism maintains that Jews who do not live in the Jewish state are in exile. There is no escaping that simple allegation, which must call into question that facile affirmation of Zionism central to American Judaism. Zionism further declares that Jews who do not live in the State of Israel must aspire to migrate to that nation or, at the very least, raise their children as potential emigrants. On that position, American Judaism chokes. Zionism, moreover, holds that all Jews must concede, indeed affirm, the centrality of Jerusalem and of the State of Israel in the life of Jews throughout the world. Zionism draws the necessary consequence that Jews who live outside of the State of Israel are in significant ways less "good Jews" than the ones who live there. Now all of these positions, commonplace in Israeli Zionism and certainly accepted in benign verbal formulations to be sure by American Jews, contradict the simple facts of the situation of American Jews and their Judaism. First, they do not think that they are in exile. Their Judaism makes no concession on that point. Second, they do not have the remotest thought of emigrating from America to the State of Israel. That is so, even though in ceremonial occasions, they may not protest when Israelis declare that to be their duty. Third, they may similarly make a ritual obeisance to carry the corollary of the peripherality of the diaspora in general and of the mighty community of American Jews in particular.

In many ways, these Jews, every day of their lives, relive the terror-filled years in which European Jews were wiped out, and every day, they do something about it. It is as if people spent their lives trying to live out a cosmic myth and, through rites of expiation and regeneration, accomplished the goal of purification and renewal. Access to the life of feeling and experience—to the way of life that made one distinctive without leaving the person terribly different from everybody else—emerged in the Judaic system of Holocaust and Redemption. The Judaism of Holocaust and Redemption presents an immediately accessible message, cast in extreme emotions of terror and triumph, its round of endless activity demanding only spare time. That Judaism realizes, in a poignant way, the conflicting demands of Jewish Americans to be intensely Jewish, but only once in a while, providing a means of expressing difference in public and in politics, while not exacting much of a cost in meaningful everyday difference from others.

This brings me back to my theory. What works? Enchantment works because it refers to experience we have had, and what rite does not transform fails because it has no field for its magnetic magic. Some words evoke worlds; others do not, because some words refer to worlds we know, while others speak of things we cannot recognize or identify. The individual in family understands life as metaphor. The family, as part of community within the realm of religion, does not. Corporate Israel exists in other dimensions, but not in the religious one. "Israel" forms a metaphor for a social entity of a particular order. But if our experience of being "Israel" does not correspond to the prevailing metaphor, expressed by its rites and prayers, then those rites and prayers will not change us. Then, rites and prayers that evoke a different experience of "being Israel" will prove effective. Now, to the coexistence of the two Judaisms, can I explain which one works when it does, and does not work when it fails? My theory is simple.

Words work when the imagination makes them work; in our minds, we make and therefore remake our world. Those words, that in their primary propositions do retain powerful appeal, address a circumstance that makes them welcome. The words that leave us Jews, in general, untouched and make no difference in shaping our world, do not. Words enchant in one setting, bore in another, because of circumstance in which they are recited and the context in life's experience in which they are heard, not because of their propositions.

I see two fundamental reasons for the present state of affairs, which finds the religion, Judaism, intensely affective in the private life and remarkably irrelevant to the public. The one reason is the prevailing attitude toward religion and its correct realm; the other is the Jews' reading of their experience of the twentieth century, which has defined, as the paramount mode of interpreting social experience, a paradigm other than that deriving from the life of that Israel that is the holy people of mind and imagination, and therefore, also of sanctification and salvation. Let me explain what I mean by the first of the two, the definition of the proper place of religion in public and political life.

We first of all turn outward when we ask why the bifurcation between the personal and the familial, subjected to the Judaism of the Dual Torah, perceived as religion, and the public and civic, governed by the Judaism of Holocaust and Redemption, perceived as politics. For the explanation lies in the definition of permissible difference in North America and the place of religion in that difference. Specifically, in North American society, defined as it is by Protestant conceptions, it is permissible to be different in religion, and religion is a matter of what is personal and private. Hence Judaism, as a religion, encompasses what is personal and familial. The Jews, as a political entity, then put forth a separate system—one that concerns not religion, which is not supposed to intervene in political action, but public policy. Judaism, in public policy, produces political action in favor of the State of Israel, or Soviet Jewry, or other important matters of the corporate community. Judaism, in private, affects the individual and the family and is not supposed

Are Jews Religious?

to play a role in politics at all. That pattern conforms to the Protestant model of religion, and the Jews have accomplished conformity to it by the formation of two Judaisms. A consideration of the Protestant pattern, which separates not the institutions of Church from the activities of the state but the entire public polity from the inner life, will show us how to make sense of the presence of the two Judaisms of North America.

Here in Protestant North America, people commonly see religion as something personal and private; prayer, for example, therefore speaks for the individual. No wonder then that those enchanted words and gestures that, for their part, Jews adopt transform the inner life, recognize life's transitions and turn them into rites of passage. It is part of a larger prejudice that religion and rite speak to the heart of the particular person. What can be changed by rite, then, is first of all, personal and private, not social, not an issue of culture, not affective in politics, not part of the public interest. What people do when they respond to religion, therefore, affects an interior world—a world with little bearing on the realities of public discourse: what, in general terms, should we do about nuclear weapons, or in terms of Judaism, how we should organize and imagine society. The transformations of religion do not involve the world, or even the self as representative of other selves, but mainly the individual at the most unique and unrepresentative. If God speaks to me, in particular, then the message by definition is mine—not someone else's. Religion, the totality of these private messages (within the present theory), therefore does not make itself available for communication in public discourse, and that by definition, too. Religion plays no public role. It is a matter not of public activity but of what people happen to believe or do in private, a matter mainly of the heart.

The Judaism of the Dual Torah forms the counterpart to religion in the Protestant model, affecting home, family, and private life. The Judaism of Holocaust and Redemption presents the counterpart to religion in the civil framework, making an impact upon public life and policy within the distinctive Jewish community of North America. The relationships between the two Judaisms prove parlous and uneven, since the Judaism of home and family takes second place in public life of Jewry; and public life is where the action takes place in that community. Not only so, but the Judaism of the Dual Torah makes powerful demands on the devotee (for example requiring him or her to frame emotions within a received model of attitudes and appropriate feelings). The Judaism of Holocaust and Redemption, by contrast, provides ready access to emotional or political encounters, easily available to all by definition. The immediately accessible experiences of politics predominate. The repertoire of human experience in the Judaism of the Dual Torah, by contrast, presents as human options the opposite of the immediate. In that Judaism, Jews receive and use the heritage of human experience captured, as in amber, in the words of the Dual Torah. That is why, in public life, Jews focus such imaginative energies as they generate upon "the Holocaust," and they center their eschatological fantasies on the "beginning of our redemption" in the State of Israel. Two competing Judaisms, the one that works at home, the other in public, therefore co-exist on an unequal basis, because the one appeals to easily imagined experience, the other to the power of will to translate and transform the here and the now into something other.

The Judaism of the Holocaust and Redemption, with its focus upon the out-there of public policy and its present paramountcy, offers a world of nightmares made of words. Its choice of formative experiences and its repertoire of worthwhile human events impose upon Jews two devilish enchantments. First, the message of Holocaust and Redemption is that difference is not destiny but disaster if one trusts the Gentiles. Second, the media of Holocaust and Redemption, political action, letters to public figures, and pilgrimages to grisly places, leave the inner life untouched but distorted. Being Jewish in that Judaism generates fear and distrust of the other, but it does not compensate by an appeal to worth and dignity for the self. The Judaism of Holocaust and Redemption leaves the life of individual and family untouched and unchanged. But people live at home and in family. Consequently, the Judaism of Holocaust and Redemption, in ignoring the private life, makes trivial the differences that separate Jew from Gentile. People may live a private life of utter neutrality, untouched by the demands of the faith, while working out a public life of acute segregation. The Judaism of Holocaust and Redemption turns on its head the wise policy of the reformers and enlightened of the early nineteenth century: a Jew at home, a citizen out there. Now, it is an undifferentiated American at home, a Jew in the public polity.

The Judaism of the Dual Torah, for its part, proves equally insufficient. Its address in here, to the self and family, to the near-exclusion of the world beyond, leaves awry its fundamental mythic structure, which appeals to history and the end of time, to sanctification and the worth of difference. Viewed whole, each of its components at the passage of life and the passing of one's own life—the disposition of birth, marriage, aging, for example—the encounter with difference makes sense only in that larger context of public policy. Separating the private and familial from the public and communal distorts the Judaism of the Dual Torah. Ignoring the individual and the deeply felt reality of the home leaves the Judaism of Holocaust and Redemption strangely vacant, and in the end, a babble of tear-producing but unfelt words, a manipulation of emotions for a transient moment. The Judaism of the Holocaust and Redemption is romantic. The Judaism of the Dual Torah accomplishes the permanent wedding of Israel, the Jewish people, to God. The one is for hotels, the other for the home. But both Judaisms speak to our divided heart today. It is time for mending.

Chapter 18

Why are Jewish Neo-Cons Atheists?

Did you ever wonder why Jewish neo-conservative thinkers never argue "from" Judaism in the way in which Michael Novak argues from Roman Catholicism and Richard Neuhaus argues from Lutheran Christianity? That is to say, Judaism never forms a point of departure. Judaism never defines a court of appeal. For the Jewish neo-cons, Judaism simply does not exist. They do not despise the Judaic religious tradition and its intellectual heritage. They simply ignore it. For the Jewish neo-cons, religion may serve valid purposes; it is instrumental, it may even be beautiful; it forms no intellectual reality from which, or even against which, to mount sustained thought.

I cannot explain why, because I am not a neo-con, although I am Jewish. Quite to the contrary, I was a conservative before I knew it, and stayed a Democrat long after voting for Republicans (but made the move in 1968 anyhow). When I was a Henry Fellow at Oxford University thirty-five years ago, I discovered that I was a conservative, not a liberal, and certainly not a socialist. As a Jew, the discovery surprised me. What I found was that the British Left in the early fifties was anti-American, the Right was pro-American, and I was an American. We were just emerging from the Korean War, which, I firmly believed, had saved South Korea from Communist aggression. But the Left in Oxford told me that we were the aggressors and should pay reparations to North Korea. These same folk had just come back from an international Youth Festival in Bucharest and brought with them other wonders and marvels to behold.

So shortly after arrival in September 1953, I located the Oxford University Blue Ribbon Society, the elite (so they told me) of the Conservatives, and for their magazine I wrote "Youth Festival in Bucharest: A Study in Fatuity." For my efforts, I got roundly abused by the Socialists and happily joined the fray. I defended not what was then called MacCarthyism but the view that Communist espionage presented a serious problem to Western security. I pointed to the Soviet domination of eastern Europe and threat to Germany. In these and other ways, I found a comfortable position in the Conservative side of Oxford politics in that interesting year. When I came home, it was, of course, as a Democrat, but a conservative one. I began voting for Republicans, and by the mid-1960s, the identification with the Republican party was complete. I began reading, then writing for, the *National Review* long before Viet Nam got rough, and I identified with the politics outlined by William F. Buckley, Jr., long, long before Norman Podhoretz had broken ranks.

I tell this brief story to indicate that, although I am a Jew and a conservative, I am not a neo-conservative. Since people generally think that neo-conservatives are Jewish intellectuals who have given up on the Left, it is important to set forth one's own credentials, especially since one trait of the Jewish neo-cons strikes me as profoundly hostile to conservativism in culture.

That is their utterly tone-deaf audience to the religion, Judaism. While paying respect to religion as instrumentally useful, the Jewish neo-cons maintain a vigorous apathy toward Judaism. We see this, every month, in *Commentary*, which while describing itself as

Why are Jewish Neo-Cons Atheists?

somehow connected to the Jewish world, represents the Judaic life of intellect by disdain and silence. That is not a new policy, to be sure. Even in the late 1940s, the great rabbi-intellectual, Milton Steinberg, dismissed *Commentary* as utterly hostile to the rich intellectual life of Judaism. It was true then, when *Commentary* belonged to the Left, and it is equally true now, with *Commentary* a bulwark of conservatism in international and social policy.

Just now, I asked myself why it should be the case that, while the Jewish conservatives (not neo-conservatives) of an earlier generation, represented by Will Herberg and Seymour Siegel, should have lived out a rich affirmation of the Judaic religious tradition and, themselves, helped enrich the Judaic intellectual tradition, the Jewish neo-cons want nothing to do with either religion or religious intellectual life when these are framed by Judaism. The occasion was a letter from Sidney Hook, whom I have admired my whole life.

He had sent me a brilliant article on the conflict between Communist party membership and the possibility of participating in universities as they flourish in the West. I read it and sent it on to the *Providence Journal* in hope that they would understand from it why Brown University should not co-operate with the KGB's Institute of the USA and Canada, with Rostock University in East Germany, and with various other Communist centers of higher learning and research— and then say so. Then, I thanked Professor Hook and, by way of reply, sent him a small monograph of mine, *The Making of the Mind of Judaism.*

The choice of the book was not without consideration. It is a work addressed to a problem of philosophy, signalled, to be sure, by my theft of the title of the great work by Randall. I wanted to know the relationship between the logic of intelligible discourse in the rabbinic texts of late antiquity and the conceptual limitations imposed by the dominant logic upon the minds shaped by that logic. The work analyzes types of logical cogency and argument, asking how one sentence joins another into an intelligible proposition, and how intelligible propositions yield syllogisms, and the equals of "one and one equals two." Now, the book may not accomplish its goals, and it certainly will not teach any logic to any second year philosophy student. But it does address a question a great philosophical mind like Hook should appreciate. Not only so, but the book purports to answer the question of why science did not develop in Judaism—that is, a typical question in the great tradition of Max Weber: why no capitalism in China or India or Judaism?

Explaining why he could not be bothered to read the book, Hook replied to me, "With respect to Jewish or Judaic learning and lore, because of the primitive Jewish education to which I was exposed in the Brooklyn slum in which I grew up, I am an *haaretz* [ignoramus]. There was never time to make it up, although I read avidly in the history of the Jews and one time the English and German translations of the books of Josephus, who fascinated me."

The Jewish study Hook found worth pursuing was then the historical and the secular—not the holy books, but the one extant secular writing of ancient Jewish life, Josephus's histories. Given the majestic voyage Hook undertook, from the Left to the Right, given the man's remarkable capacity to learn and grow through life, his dismissal of Judaic intellectual life ("there was never time to make it up") is remarkable. It makes us wonder how someone who could rethink everything else would not ask himself whether, in his original exposure to the Judaic tradition, he might have missed something important.

I point to Hook, not because he is exceptional, but because he is quite exemplary of the attitude toward the religion, Judaism characteristic of the Jewish neoconservatives, their writings and the magazines, platforms, and foundations they control. The contrast between *National Review*, with its regular page devoted to religion (now edited by Dr. John Richard Neuhaus), and *Commentary*, with never a word on Judaism, stands for much else. Why has the encounter with conservatism, with its profound appreciation for Christianity (particularly Roman Catholic Christianity) not as useful, but as true, left an entire cohort of Jewish intellectuals indifferent to Judaism? I think the answers will vary from case to case. In the instance of Hook, he went from his Jewish roots to philosophy. He did not despise; he merely dismissed his encounter with the relics of the mind of Judaism, and he never went back to look again. He concluded that Judaic thought was intellectually consequential, perhaps an embarrassment. As he moved from Left to Right, he reconsidered every judgment but that one.

Norman Podhoretz had a far superior Jewish education, studying in his college years at Jewish Theological Seminary of America. I remember that, when he was chosen editor of *Commentary*, the fact that he had a Jewish education and was supposed to be able even to read Hebrew was cited as reason for celebration; it was an element in his portfolio. Podhoretz quickly disappointed those who thought exposure to learning at JTSA would make much difference. He removed the regular stigmata of Judaic writing that the magazine had long featured, e.g., a monthly column, "Cedars of Lebanon," of Judaic classical prose. He dismissed all of the contributors of Judaic articles; in the 1950s, despite the generally sound critique of Steinberg, the magazine published articles of classic and enduring Value, (for example, important papers by Heschel and Buber). He printed occasional papers of great value by Gershom G. Scholem and Jacob Katz, a regular column of exceptional acuity by Robert Alter on Jewish literature (for literature, like history, is kosher because it is secular), and that was that. Not a single Judaic religious thinker has been published in *Commentary* in a quarter of a century. *Commentary* is Jewish, but never Judaic. Indeed, apart from intense interest in Israeli matters, even the episodes of serious Jewish, if not Judaic, writing decline in frequency.

Anything Jewish may find its place in the worldview of the neo-cons of Jewish origin, history, sociology, literature, politics—anything except religion. That seems to me anomalous, and I point to the anomaly. But I can't really explain it, because I am not a neo-con. I was a conservative when Hook was a left wing Democrat and when Podhoretz had not yet climbed off the barricades and broken ranks and made it; so, although Jewish, I can't pretend to know how their minds work.

All I know is that, when it comes to the rich and sanctifying Judaic religious life, with its sophisticated intellectual heritage of reflection and rigorous thought, these people stand at one with the Left, in unity with the learned despisers of religion. Their conservatism has not yet fulfilled itself.

Chapter 19

Should Jews Celebrate Bastille Day?

No, we Jews gained nothing on Bastille Day, but we lost a great deal. So, I don't think we have anything to celebrate in the French Revolution. It was very bad for the Jews. Let me explain why.

The complex situation of Judaism now in modern times, with its intersecting but distinct Judaic systems for the private life and the public square, responds to the social world in which Jews live. Religion, narrowly defined, is deemed personal and individual and familial. Politics is public and shared and corporate. The nation-state that required a common language and shared politics, that fostered a uniform culture among diverse groups, that reduced all persons to the common status of citizen, accorded no public recognition to the importance of cultural or religious difference. And that conception of religion as private, the public square as neutral, emerged from the French revolution.

If you were not of the religion or color or ethnic origin or race of the majority, you would find a place within the majority by emphasizing the common responsibilities of citizenship. But the points of difference must be subordinated and would be tolerated in private. So, religious difference—which could not be erased or overcome—would be forced out of the public square, and a civil religion substituted within it.

That accounts for the shape of Judaisms in the twentieth century in the Western democracies. The policy for all diverse groups would be, in theory at least, essentially the same. We may paraphrase the way in which a principal figure in the French Revolution put matters as they pertained to the Jews, "To the Jews as citizens, everything; to Judaism as corporate community, nothing." To this statement of public policy, a Jewish thinker responded with what defines the settlement that Jews adopted for themselves from the late eighteenth century onward: "Be a Jew at home, a human being when you go forth."

This peculiar political settlement worked out in the West through the differentiation of religion and politics; the holy and the secular came about in the aftermath of protracted and bloody religious wars in the Reformation. Not only so, but the nurture of a value-free public policy and the development of a world of exchange that was neutral to cultural and religious difference responded to the rise of a new order of capitalist economics, which required growing markets and flourished only with the interchangeability of persons and products alike, attained through uniformity and rationality in not only production and consumption but also law, society, and politics.

Under such conditions, the recognition in public policy accorded that difference endangered the public order on the one side and impeded the progress of the formation of wealth on the other. But in the long centuries before the formation in the West of the capitalistic mode of social organization on the one side and the political neutrality as to difference in religion and culture on the other, quite different conditions for a very long span of time, back to remote antiquity, characterized the social order.

Specifically, the division between the private and the public, the religious and the political, was unknown. People took for granted that one's religion was the same as one's ethnic identity, and one's ethnic identity was the same as one's nationality. Instead of nation-states, with cultural uniformity in language and culture such as we know today, the political entities of Europe, Asia, and North Africa encompassed varieties of groups held together in multi-cultural empires.

When, as was the case very commonly, a given territory encompassed much linguistic and cultural diversity, the economy would afford specialization to the different groups. In ancient times, for example, the Canaanite was the trader, the Phoenician the international merchant, and the Jews in the land of Israel (later, Palestine) were farmers and soldiers. The local, subsistence economies did not require interchangeability of persons and products, the mass production and consumption of goods and services, or the rationalization of the formation of wealth. Instead of the notion of large markets, people thought in terms of local bazaars; in place of large-scale enterprise (though there was such) aimed at the systematic and orderly creation of wealth, people looked for the main chance and the one-shot deal.

So, the economic impulse for the reduction of difference to the private and personal realm and uniformity in public policy did not affect the framing of policy for religion and culture.

Politics, too, accorded to difference an important place. Indeed, in the organization of large empires, properly manipulated difference served the interests of those who held power. For by protecting the rights of small groups, organizers of empires could and did win loyalty and willing assent to their exercise of large-scale authority. Coercion served much less well than obedience, and fealty best of all. According to the political myth characteristic of much of the world of diversity, such as was comprised by Europe, the Middle East, and North Africa—where Judaism (and Christianity and Islam flourished)—personal fealty, concrete and palpable, and not abstract loyalty to the nation-state, defined by language and culture, governed. That is why people, for the long centuries prior to the advent of the nation-state in the late eighteenth century, understood that various groups followed their own laws and customs but owed allegiance to a ruler in common. Consequently, an empire would encompass a variety of languages, religions, and cultures, and each group formed a self-sustaining social entity.

The division of a person's life into that of the citizen and the private individual serves now; but under the conditions that prevailed in Europe, North Africa, and the Middle East for millennia before the nineteenth century, it contradicted public policy. That policy, as we realize, never contemplated the homogenization of populations. True, if people worshipped a god deemed evil or false, they might be wiped out, as Christians wiped out "pagans" in their conquest of much of Europe and as Muslims destroyed idolators, according the right of subordinated status to Jews and Christians in their conquest of the Middle East, North Africa, and the Iberian peninsula.

But the great empires took for granted that they would encompass and tolerate difference, and society was so ordered as to preserve, in stable hierarchy, the layers and levels of difference, whether the difference be marked by religion, culture, language, food, education, profession and craft and economic status, clothing—or all of them all together.

And that meant for Judaism a world in which everything held together under the aspect of Heaven. If a person were a Jew, then he or she ate food identified as Jewish, spoke or, at least, used for culture and religion a language particular to Jews (Hebrew, and in Europe for nearly a thousand years, Yiddish—that is, the Jewish language), was educated in the traditions of learning of Judaism, might well wear clothing that marked the person as a Jew, practiced professions or businesses that were generally assigned to Jews, lived within a political framework comprising mostly Jews, and in general, like numerous other ethnic-cultural-religious subsets of society, formed a free-standing and essentially autonomous social system. Under such conditions, distinguishing religion from politics and the private from the communal would have proven just as puzzling as treating the two as one, as our own society does.

As a matter of fact, from the most ancient times, empires were polyglot and multi-cultural. Once a conquering people passed the frontiers of its own country, it faced the task of governing foreigners. Seeking allies wherever he could, a king would be glad to join with lesser powers and add their armies to his own. To do so, he might offer to protect established practices and rites. The Romans, for example, did exactly that with the Jews when they came into the Near East and made an ally out of the Judean State in what later was to be called Palestine. They guaranteed Jews' rights of free practice of their culture and local autonomy, as allies of Rome. Those rights persisted from the second century B.C. to the fifth century C.E., when the now-Christian Roman empire abrogated many of them. But the basic policy of accommodating important difference—even at the price of subordinated status—remained firm for the whole of western history to 1789.

And through the Near and Middle East and North Africa from ancient times to the advent of the nation-state, the essentials of the tolerant attitude that favored (whether of right or of necessity) a pluralistic culture, religion, and society dictated public policy for many centuries—until the French revolution. So, what is there to celebrate?

Contrast the accommodation, even tolerance, of genuine difference characteristic of the great empires before the French revolution with the pseudo-liberalism of a tolerance that denied important difference characteristic of the French revolution, and you will answer: Nothing to celebrate, not today on Bastille Day! It was a disaster for the great, historical religious traditions of the West, including Judaism; and it also was a political calamity for the Jewish people.

It made Jews claim they weren't different, though they had always been—that was deeply characteristic of the French revolution. So, for Jews, there is nothing to celebrate, not on Bastille Day. The French Revolution went on to murder nuns and priests and to destroy churches; the world has recognized that. But it also proceeded to de-Judaize the Jews, to define the terms of their existence in ways that denied the Jews their right to be themselves.

The world should recognize that, too—beginning with the Jews.

The Left has not loved us, and the German National Socialist Workers Party was not the first to say so.

Chapter 20

Is America the Promised Land for Jews?

It's time to say that America is a better place to be a Jew than Jerusalem. If ever there was a promised land, we Jewish Americans are living in it. Here, Jews have flourished, not alone in politics and the economy, but in matters of art, culture, and learning. Jews feel safe and secure here in ways that they do not and cannot in the State of Israel. And they have found an authentically Jewish voice—their own voice—for their vision of themselves.

That is not to say the long centuries of wandering have ended. God alone knows the future. But for here, now, and for whatever future anyone can foresee, America has turned out to be our promised land.

And that creates a problem, because American Jews are supposed to feel a bit guilty about living here. They're expected to fear for their future and take for granted that a full Jewish life is to be lived only in Jerusalem—that is, in the State of Israel.

Some Israelis tell American Jews that America, like the fleshpots of Egypt, is no place for a Jew; we're all going to die in gas chambers singing Christmas carols. The message is that we are not supposed to feel secure, because anti-Semitism will catch up to us, as it has to Jews everywhere else throughout history.

Meanwhile, the story goes, we're all "assimilating"; we've stopped being Jewish. Nearly six million Jews today—they tell us—are all marrying Gentiles and jumping off the sinking ship of Judaism. I, for one, haven't yet felt the nudge of the iceberg, and I don't think I'm singing on the deck of the *Titanic*. I think the Jews have built a Jewish life in America that can last, and that, even now, is giving plenty of proof of stability and human value.

The truth is that Jews can make it in freedom. America, the freest and most open society Jews have ever known, is not only good for the Jews, but better for the Jews than the State of Israel—and not because we prefer the fleshpots or even like singing "Silent Night."

First, are we assimilating? I think not. We're changing. But change is not assimilation—it's change. We're different from our grandparents. Our children will be different from us. But the emblems are multiplying of a highly cohesive Jewish community with traits that mark us as distinctive.

Fifteen years ago, Jewish sociologists who studied the question announced that Jews were disappearing because they weren't having enough children. This prophecy has been made by each generation of Jews since our patriarch, Abraham, 3,500 years ago. Failing to foresee the birth of Isaac, Abraham thought that Eliezer of Damascus, who wasn't Jewish, would be his heir. When the sociologists told us we were on our way out, the Israelis argued that, if we wanted a Jewish future, we had to emigrate. But it turns out that the disappearing American Jew is going to be around for a while, because the sociologists got their numbers wrong. Intermarriage, so it seems at the moment, is a demographic plus, not a minus. The reason, surveys show, is that the non-Jewish partner often either converts or identifies with the Jewish community, and at least half of the children do.

Second, are the "goyim" out to get us? There is anti-Semitism, among other hatreds, in this country.

But every public opinion poll confirms the impression given by noting that no fewer than seven United States senators are Jewish (six with the death Friday of Edward Zorinsky of Nebraska)—7 percent of the Senate from only 2 percent of the population—and that countless other Jewish public officials of both major parties serve in high office in state and local government. Jews are an accepted group, flowing in the mainstream of American life.

A good measure of anti-Semitism takes the temperature of the community from within. There we see collective affirmation of Jewish existence. Synagogues and all sorts of Jewish organizations and institutions thrive. Jews in every walk of life, in the military, in large corporations and universities, government and public institutions—everywhere Jews make their way—face little or no hostility.

So when Israelis tell us we have to emigrate and "make aliyah"—meaning, ascent to live in the Holy Land, lest we assimilate and die (or both)—they appeal to an evil nightmare, one that gives little sign of coming true.

The immigrant generations of Jews built good lives in America, and their great grandchildren are still Jewish. True enough, they are Jewish in ways different from what their great grandparents understood. For example, they speak unaccented American, not Yiddish; they ordinarily do not observe dietary taboos, and they live pretty much within the calendar that governs everyone else. But they also maintain the marks of a highly distinctive community. Every social study has turned up strong evidence of Jews' communal cohesiveness.

The most perverse argument made is that Americans must settle in Israel if they want to have a Jewish future, because the benign, welcoming climate here is destructive to Jewish culture. Unless we all live in little ghettos, the reasoning goes, we're going to disappear.

Jews can maintain themselves only in a segregated circumstance, and so the state of Israel offers the only hope. But where does this bizarre argument come from?

When the political Zionist movement began in the nineteenth century, the projected Jewish state was supposed to serve as haven for those Jews who wished to go there or had no other choice. What would happen to the others was not quite clear. Some thought they should assimilate, so that pretty much all Jews would live in the Jews' state. Others projected that state as a "spiritual center" that would serve as a light to Israel, the Jewish people, wherever they lived, and even to the nations.

Later on, with the success of the State of Israel, a new claim came forth. Only in the State of Israel can Jews live a "full Jewish life," and still further, only in the State of Israel can Jews have a future. Jews in the diaspora (Israelis are too polite to call it "the Exile") will wither and fade.

What that has come to mean is simple. As an Israeli professor of political science from Tel Aviv University said to me, "If you are right, we are wrong." What he meant is that if Jews in the United States give evidence of sustaining a long future, then there is no "need" to build or live in the Jewish state. Consequently, anyone who maintained that Jews in other countries can succeed in maintaining their distinctive community and faith became "anti-Zionist" or even "anti-Jewish."

What I hear in the odd turning of ideology is that Jews cannot live in a free and open society, that Judaism required the ghetto, and that freedom—an absolute good for everyone else—is bad for the Jews. What a remarkable judgment upon the human meaning of Judaism!

So, let's turn the matter around and ask whether Zionism has kept its promises for the Jews. Where, really, is it better to be a Jew?

Zionism promised that the Jewish state would be a spiritual center for the Jewish people. But today, in all the Jewish world, who, as a matter of Jewish sentiment or expression, reads an Israeli book, or looks at an Israeli painting, or goes to an Israeli play, or listens to Israeli music? Apart from some fine fiction, Israeli art and creative life have made only a slight impact on American Jews. They do not look to Tel Aviv for stimulation or for imagination. And throughout the Jewish world, people do look to America. They hire rabbis educated in America. They follow patterns of community organization pioneered in America.

Then what about Jewish scholarship? There, at least, from the Hebrew-speaking country, should come light and insight. In fact, Jerusalem is no "light to the Gentiles," or even to the Jews.

The not-very-well-kept secret is that, except in a few areas of natural strength, such as archaeology of the land of Israel or Hebrew language studies, Israeli scholarship is pretty dull. After Martin Buber, not a single major Israeli thinker has made a mark outside the intellectual village of Jerusalem. After Gershom Scholem, not a single Israeli scholar in the study of Judaism has won any audience at all outside of the State of Israel. Everyone can boast about locals. But who, today, is listening?

No historians, no philosophers in Judaic studies have a hearing overseas. Israeli scholarship boasts no social scientists working on Jewish materials in a way that interests anyone but Jews. Israeli scholarship in Judaic studies is provincial, erudite, unimaginative, remarkably unproductive—just a lot of dull-witted fact-mongering by third-rate academic politicians. The level of academic discourse is easily grasped when you realize that character-assassination has replaced criticism of ideas.

And, everywhere in the Jewish world, Jewish scholarship produced in America is read. Books of Jewish history, religion, literature and philosophy written by Jewish Americans appear in all European languages.

American Jewish theologians led in the Jewish-Christian ecumenical movement. Israelis take a second place. And here we do debate ideas.

Then, what about living in the State of Israel to recharge our Jewish batteries? It's got wonderful hotels, great scenery, first-rate tours, and Jewish everything. It's like what they say about New York—a great place to visit.

Beyond that, though, world Jewry has voted with its feet. When the Algerian Jews were driven out of Algeria, the French government offered to provide them with the same settlement aid to go to Haifa or Lyon. Most chose France.

When Soviet Jews leave for the free West, some choose the State of Israel. Most don't.

More Israelis live in the United States than in Jerusalem. Enough said.

What about the political change the State of Israel has brought about for world Jewry?

No doubt, the sight of a Jewish state defending Jewish lives moves us all. Would that it had come a decade sooner!

But Entebbe is not the whole story, or even a big part of it. Israelis tell us that they have made the Jewish people independent for the first time in 2,000 or more years; now there is not only a Jewish state, but the Jewish people, as a political entity, make their own decisions and are able to dictate their own fate and future.

Would that it were so! In fact, the State of Israel is a client state, not Sparta or Athens either. Having priced itself out of independence in economic terms, and because of recurring wars, the State of Israel depends upon a generous America. That's perfectly natural in a world divided between the superpowers. But it does not add up to independence.

I, for one, am glad that the State of Israel has allied itself so closely with our country. I think it's good for this country to have one really strong, reliable, and stable ally in the Middle East. But it's hard to see how Israeli dependence on American military and economic support squares with the claim that Jews, if they live in the State of Israel, are really all that independent. I'm not even sure what independence can mean.

Then, what about religion? At least, here, the Jewish state should have kept its promise.

In some ways it has. I cannot imagine anything more beautiful than the Sabbath in Jerusalem or the pilgrim festivals in Galilee. Nor is there more pleasure in this life than attending a worship service in an Israeli synagogue where the people believe with all their hearts the truth of every word of worship, which they understand and fully grasp. And if you want to see a national society that treats the aged with dignity and children with unrepressed love, go to the State of Israel. They even know how to bury their dead without sentimentality and with honesty. In these and other ways, they have human lessons to teach us all. Israelis are wonderful to young children and the aged. It's just the middle years, between childhood and old age, where they find it hard to sort things out.

One thing they have not yet solved is how to provide religious freedom for Jews. For instance, as a Conservative rabbi, I have no standing in the state of Israel—unless I accept the status of a heretic. The state supports and recognizes only Orthodoxy, and Orthodoxy of a peculiarly primitive character, at that. State-Orthodox rabbis just now have told women to stay away from burials of the dead because they are "impure." So much for state-Orthodoxy in the state of Israel. Reform, Conservative, and Reconstructionist as well as Orthodox Jews enjoy religious equality in America, but not in the state of Israel. In sheer numbers, these non-Orthodox Judaisms dominate world Jewry, but the state of Israel treats them as heresies.

Not a single Israeli rabbi or other religious figure can claim to exercise moral authority outside the state of Israel. In fact, beyond the limited circles of Orthodoxy within the state of Israel, not one religious figure has an audience of any kind. The Israeli rabbinate lacks all moral standing in the diaspora for Reform and Conservative Jews, who make up the vast majority of Jews in the United States and Canada.

So much for being a Jew in the state of Israel. Here, in the diaspora, we can be what we want, when we want—from nothing to everything, all the time or once in a while. Freedom is nice, too. And this really has become a free country for us Jews. It wasn't always that way. It may not always be that way. But let's stop denying what, at least now, it is.

For American Jews—now Jewish Americans—the American dream has come true. I wonder how many Israelis think the Zionist one has come true, too.

Chapter 21

The Jews as the Generic Minority Group

We Jews are like everybody else, only more so. There is such a thing as a generic minority group, and if you want to know how to define the genus, just generalize on our traits as a community. For we are the most perfect species of the genus, "generic minority group."

Imagine a world made of "we," the few, arrayed against "them," everybody else. "Our" group is made of people marked by a common trait. We make much of that trait; it is what sets us apart, marking us as different (We think better; they think inferior). Life inside our group is tight and warm. We take care of each other. True, we also talk harshly and sharply to one another, occasionally even calling an insider by an epithet that, used by outsiders, gives offense. But with others like ourselves, we feel comfortable and secure.

The outside world is another matter. When we go among "them" (that is, everyone else), we have to watch our words and our ways. We have to use public language, not the in-slang of the group. We demand respect for our group, recognition for ourselves. Inside, we argue freely. Outside, we pretend to unanimity. Inside, we think the unthinkable. Outside, we profess permitted thoughts alone. For the world—so we see it—is hostile, and we are beleaguered. The outside threat to our security and continuity requires defense of high walls—walls in the imagination, to be sure, but nonetheless, tall and sheltering.

You see, we really live in two worlds, one at home, the other at large. In the other America, we feel normal, ourselves, whatever that is supposed to be. In the alien America, we are marked as different. Our ideal is to be whatever we want, whenever we want: different when we want, the same when we choose. But in reality, we are only and always different.

Sometimes we hate the thing that makes us different, whether heritage or gender, skin tone or place of origin. Other times we exalt in it. When we hate ourselves for being different, it is with venom. When we love the difference, it is to excess. So too with our leaders. We admire those who have made it in the outside world, but then the leadership of leaders from the periphery underlines the bad underside of difference and makes us hate ourselves still more. And for their part, these leaders from the periphery exercise control within, while claiming exemption in the world beyond from the penalties for difference. So the tensions grow; the turmoil boils.

If you can imagine life in a laager of the mind, you can construct for yourself the world mentally made up by what I call "the generic minority group." For in American society at large, are not a few groups that see themselves under siege—and expect members of those groups to live that way. The generic minority group imposes censorship on the group, self-censorship on the individual. Say what you will in the privacy of the group, so long as you don't let the outsider hear. Admit no fault; concede no failing; defend all positions at any cost. What makes us different makes us beautiful; absence of that same trait makes them less. We can say and do to one another whatever we will, but God save the outsider who tries to say, in friendship, what to one another we say with hatred. We are fastidious; they are gross. We are soulful; they

The Jews as the Generic Minority Group

are brutish. We are smart; they are there to be manipulated. We support our own; they are out to get us. Imagine such a world—for it is round about us.

When blacks call one another "nigger" or Jews use "kike"; when Greek millionaires support Tsongas or Dukakis because they're Greek; when black politicians will not criticize their "own kind" even while privately despising one another; when, as with the Jews on the state of Israel, insiders fight but pretend to present a united front to the world at large; when it's all right to say in our private language what in public cannot be said at all—these all indicate the presence of mentality of that single generic minority group, the beleaguered, the frightened, the besieged, without regard to whether the distinguishing indicative trait derives from race, creed, color, gender, or previous condition of servitude.

What all the generic minorities mistake is that inner world of fear and frenzy with the real world of prevailing indifference joined to modest curiosity. A kind of collective paranoia affects the generic minority, making it assume that people like or dislike, when in fact, they're generally indifferent. Jews worry more about what the Gentiles will think about the Jews than Gentiles ever think about the Jews. They think Gentiles treat the Jews as special, to be hated or perhaps loved, when Gentiles, in general, tend to be merely curious. The Jews are just one among a number of distinct and distinctive groups—except in their own conception. In their own imagination, they are not one among many, but the main one: us against them. And so too are all other minorities, forming this generic minority group, each one more important in its own eyes than in anyone else's.

And they make yet another mistake. They assume that, if they wanted, they could keep things to themselves. Forming in its own mind a village, a camp, a fortress, the generic minority, in fact, lives in the global village. People hear; they're curious; debate is public and cannot be kept private. Jews do not speak Yiddish or Hebrew among themselves but English, which everyone overhears. And if an article appears in a black newspaper, a good reporter in a metropolitan daily is going to pick it up. The fantasy that people can vigorously debate at home and present a united front outside conflicts with the reality of life in this country, where—to the degree that people are interested—everybody knows everybody else's business.

But the real error is not one of the *is* but of the *ought*: even if the generic minority could keep its business to itself, is it really to its advantage to do so? I think not, for three reasons.

First, rational debate on public policy always clarifies choices, weighs alternatives, allows issues to be clearly drawn. Stifling debate invites error. Fully airing issues secures for the common good whatever insight and perspective the community can find for itself.

Second, public debate strengthens the community that sustains it, because it engages a broad variety of opinion in the common good. The opposite of public debate is not chaos and public disarray, but indifference. When a small minority decides things, whether in a university, an organization, or a community, people vote with their feet. They walk away: "They decided— let them do it."

Third, this is, after all America, where we really do believe in free speech. If freedom is good for everybody, it has to be good for the generic minority too.

Mouthing such a banality might prove embarrassing, except that within the generic minority, them's fightin' words.

There, people still argue about why the community must be bound by a discipline not imposed by "outsiders," nor, of course, upon them. "We" owe it to ourselves to keep the faith, which means, always justify our side, always reject criticism or explain away flaws

The Jews as the Generic Minority Group 213

or failings others may see in us. Never give an inch of self-criticism, always grab a yard of glory. Therefore, know who is "us," and who is not. And lovingly list all the "us's"—Jews in sports, blacks in politics, women engineers—anything to break the stereotype, or reenforce it.

If you think this exercise in making up a generic minority community glib or mere fantasy, let me report things that really happened, just now, right here in Washington (and as a matter of fact, all over the Jewish world). And they happened to me. For I proudly belong to a species of the genus, minority group, the Jewish species, which is the most average and the most typical of the lot.

Last March, I asked in this space here, "Is America the promised land for Jews?" And I answered my own question: Yes, it is good to be a Jew in America, and for many reasons. Nearly all Jewish Americans agree. We know, because they vote—if not with their feet by sitting down right here and staying for a long, long while.

It was a very pro-American statement, but it got me into a lot of trouble with Jewish Americans. The reason is that I violated a language-norm of the Jewish species of the generic minority. I said in public what you're only allowed to say in private. In public, we're supposed to agree when Israelis tell us they're our "spiritual center"; we can only be true blue Jews (in their idiom, "live a full Jewish life") in Zion; we're dying out anyhow through assimilation and intermarriage, and the goyim will kill us before we die (thus my bitter "singing Christmas carols in the gas chambers")—and anyhow, we stay here only because of the fleshpots. So we're Americans by reason of leeks and onions, thus the Israeli line.

I know that Jewish Americans reject every line of the Israeli reading of their everyday destiny. They are, in the aggregate, passionately American, like everyone else. Believing with all their heart in the dogma of American exceptionalism—whatever the rule of humanity to this, this morning, we think ourselves exceptional, Jews, among other Americans, translate "promised land" into home sweet home.

Everyone thinks it. I said it.

Wham, bang! Three leading Jewish Republicans called the White House to tell the President they're mad at me, so he should not appoint me to a high federal office for which I was under consideration, so White House friends tell me. (Still, in all due pride, only three?)

Rabbis all over the country got their sermon for that week; editorialists in the Jewish press owe me a commission; I gave them something to write about.

Why all this? Because I violated the Jews' equivalent of the iron law of omerta; I told the truth in public.

So when I asked whether or not this might not be—at least for here, at least for now—the promised land, I got lots of replies. But that was not the question people answered.

Being the archetypal generic minority community, the Jews condemned not what I said ("granted you're right, we really do have a Jewish future in this country—but you shouldn't have said it"), but where I said it, or how I said it ("I like your message, but not your language"). It came down to the same thing. I said what most people agree with but don't want to have said in front of the goyim (which is to say, everybody outside the laager).

From Washington: "Don't you know the *Washington Post* is put out by a bunch of anti-Semites?"

From Jerusalem: "Say it in Hebrew, we all know. But if you say it in the *Washington Post*, the goyim will hear too."

From synagogue pulpits all over Washington—and, later on, the USA and Western Europe, so I hear: "He's right—but why did he print it there?"

But talk is cheap. Some people took action. A Zionist magazine (until February, I thought of myself as a Zionist and held a life membership in the Zionist Organization of America) for which I wrote regularly pulled an article of mine already set in type and proofread.

And that was a less amusing side to things. From the editor of *Midstream*, a journal of Jewish affairs which is published by the Jewish Agency, came this letter:

> I'm sure you are aware of the immense pleasure it gave me to print your essays, which have always seemed to me a unique fusion of erudition and sparkling incisiveness . . . But, your recent broadside against Zionism, which I understand has appeared in more than four hundred fifty newspapers, on the front page of the relevant sections, has now . . . changed your 'image' in the mind of a very broad public. From that point of view, even minor cosmetic changes in 'Two Judaisms?' [an essay of mine then in corrected galleys, scheduled for the magazine's next issue] would scarcely be enough to justify *Midstream*, which is, after all, a combat organ of the Zionist movement, in printing it. I enclose it, accordingly, with great regret, and with my assurance to you of my great esteem for your remarkable qualities.

That has to be the saddest letter ever written. I was put under administrative excommunication in reprisal, not for what I said but for saying it in the wrong place—in front of the goyim.

But anyone who wants to blame the "Zionist juggernaut" for reprisals against me errs. I'm on lots of peoples' lists of unacceptable persons, and for lots of reasons. And so is everybody else who has anything to say in Jewish affairs—if not on one list, then on some other. That's how it is in the generic minority community. For the issue is not what you say but whether you are heard; for if you are heard but "the community" cannot control you, then you form a threat. And the threat is the thing, not the occasion.

As I told the editor of *Midstream*, "Your colleagues are no worse than anyone else. If it hadn't been for this, it would have been for something else." And the lists, in Jewish agencies and institutions, seminaries and communities, that prohibit Jacob Neusner have plenty more names. I'm not the only one, though I might be on more such lists than some others, and for more (and more varied) reasons. But enough of boasting.

For the point is simple: the genus minority, species Jewish, thinks it can control and manipulate not only public discourse but, especially, its own members. The generic minority, threatened, as it feels itself to be, exercises on its "own" a kind of despotism that the generic minority could not conceivably tolerate from others. It's part of the same pattern that allows blacks to call one another "nigger," and that permits Jews to label "their own kind" "kikey"—or, if they live in Wisconsin or Rhode Island, elaborately to proclaim how much they hate "New York."

My own experience suggests that the censorship and the excommunication aim, not at me, but at others who might follow my lead. People know that if I can't print something here, I'll find a place somewhere else, because I'm not likely to be shut up. But the game's the thing: "See what we can do to him (even if it makes no difference to him), because we can and will do it to you, too." And that's another matter. Censorship of this one intimidates many others, people with more at stake, in the nature of things, than that insider-outsider with standing in the world at large and not really subject to the (imagined) discipline of "the community" anyhow.

The Jewish community in this country has got to discover America. What they have to learn is that it really is a free country.

The Jews as the Generic Minority Group

In this country, everybody lives in public—and we Jews more than most. The idea that we can conduct our affairs within a privileged sanctuary of silence, debating things by ourselves, and then presenting a united front to a hostile world, is wrong. And it's not only wrong, it's dumb.

If we do not debate freely and openly, how shall we ever know right from wrong? And what makes us think people can be kept from hearing our debates? And why would we assume that mere curiosity, generally friendly, at that, of the world at large represents a threat or a statement of hostility?

There are more reasons for free and public discourse within the Jewish community than merely the intrinsic worth of defining public policy in public.

First, the world is not all that hostile. Not everybody hates us because we're Jews, and we don't hate anybody (more or less). At home, in my own university, for local reasons, I've taken a pretty controversial stand on Brown's administration. Many people have gotten very mad at me. In seven years of leading the contrast to this particular regime, I have not once gotten a letter, signed or unsigned, of an anti-Semitic character. That's the one (and only) thing the other side has not held against me. In more general terms, people don't think they're anti-Semitic when they disagree with, or get mad as hell at, Jews. And, they're right; they're not.

Second, whether or not people hate us, we are living in a free and open society. People listen to people. When blacks won't criticize Jesse Jackson in public, but will in private, everyone in America hears about it. And why not? It's part of public life, lived by our friends and neighbors, therefore by us all. America is segregated beyond a thousand walls, but all of them, in public, are invisible.

Third, some of our business is public anyhow, like—for the Jewish species of the genus the $3 billion a year that we all think the state of Israel should continue to get to help it keep going, not to mention political support in every other way. We address the public forum with a long list of things we want. We are, therefore, part of public discourse. How can we pretend that we can stop people from tuning in on our channel?

The same is so for the blacks and all other examples of the generic minority community. Blacks come to the public forum with many important and legitimate demands. Can they deny to the same public forum the right to hear diverse opinion, coming from blacks, about what blacks think is good for blacks? Will Hispanics pretend that they have only a single interest (for example, immigration laws to ease the everyday fears of good working people) and not a multiplicity of interests and concerns? When Jews, blacks, Hispanics, and (even) women pretend to a uniformity that exists only in imagination, they confirm the one hostile judgment of the world beyond: they're really all alike, they look alike and act alike—and, therefore, can be judged alike, and not as individuals. But none of us in the generic minority world wants that. We don't want to be told we all look alike, because we don't. But then let's stop pretending we all think alike.

Perhaps a personal note makes this clear. Just now, Ella Fitzgerald told me I look just like Benny Goodman, to which I replied, "Yes, true, we really all do look alike. But to me you don't look like Dizzie Gillespie." So much for the confrontation of generic minorities: "We" are always a we to "them," and everyone else is them. Anyhow, if I had my druthers, I'd rather be mistaken for Robert Redford. Enough on the generic minority group for this morning: the lesson on self-hatred is yet to come.

Back to the centerpiece: it's O.K. to say it, but only in private (in Hebrew, not in English, in the *Washington Jewish Week*, not in the *Washington Post*, in a synagogue, not in a public speech, or wherever). I don't think that is how Jews want things. I think not, because in every other way we have rejected living in a ghetto and don't want to. Then why pretend that in selected matters we do? We talk freely about pretty much whatever we want—no more verbal people in the world, I'd say, than us—and who is going to tell us to shut up on proscribed matters?

We come from a tradition of free debate and sustained, rigorous inquiry. No question too tough, no answer too sensitive, stands in the way of the practical and applied reason of talmudic studies, for instance. Everything is open, everything up for grabs. And that is the secret of our vigorous and exciting intellectual life.

What about the argument that it's O.K. to say it in the *Washington Jewish Week*, but not in the *Washington Post*? Many rabbis wrote me that.

I don't know why. Public discourse is in the public interest, and the conception that one forum is open, another forbidden, redefines censorship in a not very subtle way. It is to say, "Write anything you want, so long as no one reads it." Or, ". . . as long as we can control who reads it." That kind of freedom of speech is really freedom to whisper—and best of all, to whisper into deaf ears.

The same goes for the argument that it's O.K. to criticize the state of Israel in Jerusalem, which I got from friends abroad. That's just a variation on the argument that the goyim might hear, so watch what you say. "Come here and say it," so they wrote. But why? You are the ones who claim to be our "spiritual center," to condemn our future and see only glory in your own. So hear a message from out here, in the periphery beyond the far horizon.

Israelis cannot have it all ways, claiming to form our center but then denying us the right to speak at all where we are and about what we think we are. And we Jews cannot have it every which way. We can't jump into debates on public policy and frame a Jewish position—and we do on a vast range of issues, and I think we should—but then, claim that on some issues public debate is forbidden.

We can't both live in an open society and also pretend that we live in a ghetto and can mumble in a private language behind the walls. We speak English, not Yiddish or Hebrew. We live wherever we want, say whatever we want, do whatever we want. That's freedom. Why, then, restrict that freedom and even imagine we can penalize those who exercise it?

For no one who condemned me for writing in the *Washington Post* and not (as some wrote from Jerusalem) in the *Jerusalem Post* (where—they said—they would agree with me and even say the same thing!) could imagine that this particular writer was going to be intimidated. The rabbis' sermons, which provided pulpit talk for weeks after my article, were not addressed to me, even though for a while, I might not have won any popularity contests in the synagogues. The rabbis addressed the people present, not to the absent ogre. And they meant to impose a kind of sanction, not on one individual, but on anyone who might go and do the same: in the full light of day talk freely and honestly about things that really count.

That's the real purpose of condemning my writing in the *Washington Post*. That stood for a kind of confidence in American freedom that some within the Jewish world do not view very fondly. What it means is that the Jews are out of control—their control. But we already are. If you want to control the Jews, rebuild the ghetto walls—because that's where you're going to have to start. Then get the government to pass laws to require all Jews to live in ghettos. While you're at it, maybe some sort of personal marking, if not a *mezuzah* on a chain, then maybe something flashy, like a yellow Star of David.

No, I think not. Faced with the implications of the policy of (self-)censorship or excommunication for truth-telling, Jews will make only one choice.

People who have managed to sustain a lively community and a vital intellectual life for more than three thousand years are not going to be intimidated. And in this country of all places, there is no way that the argument "what will the goyim say" is going to prove compelling.

Freedom is an absolute good, and that means it's good also for the Jews—and for all the other groups in the model of the generic minority.

So, that's why we're like everybody else, only more so.

Chapter 22

Self-Segregation in an Open Society?

Do members of minority groups—religious, ethnic, racial, "sexual preference," what have you—have rights of free speech when it comes to issues that matter to their particular groups? Well, not if some people can stop it.

I found that out in the columns of the *Tampa Tribune*, when a while back, I pointed out how Israeli Prime Minister Shamir said settlements in Judea and Samaria (a.k.a., the West Bank) were his government's highest priority, even if it meant losing loan guarantees to build housing for the immigrants from the former USSR. Zionism places highest priority on providing a secure homeland for all Jews who want and need it; so I said this is a betrayal of Zionism. A local rabbi responded, and there the matter ended: a disagreement publicly aired, for people to consider.

Well, not quite ended. A few days ago, I got a letter from a Jewish colleague at my university, the University of South Florida, whom I had never met: "I didn't read your letter in the *Tampa Tribune*, but I heard about it, and you shouldn't have published it there." Without regard to the merit of my proposition and argument, I was guilty of disloyalty: I didn't practice self-censorship. I broke ranks.

The burden of his message was, publish disagreement in the *Jewish Press* (a local weekly serving the

Jewish communities of the bay area, which prints plenty of ads and canned news—arguably the most trivial and boring Jewish paper in the world), but never in "public." He thinks "we Jews have to stick together," and so, we can't disagree in front of outsiders. We have to put up a united front.

Now, as a matter of fact, a healthy majority of American Jews thinks it's quite all right to disagree about anything you want, anywhere you want. A recent survey reported in the *Jerusalem Report* says 55 percent agree: it's O.K. to criticize Israel, if you want; about a third would concur with my USF colleague, and the rest have no opinion.

But when you look around, you realize that that same mentality—freedom of speech for everybody but Jews, if you're Jewish, on Jewish questions—flourishes all over the place. The generic American minority is supposed to be self-segregated.

It certainly looks as though blacks have freedom of speech on everything but questions important to blacks, on which they have to toe the line. For we don't hear much public debate from black leaders about public policy in the black community.

For instance, we had a lecture up at USF by a scholar of Afro-American studies named Jeffries, who thinks white folk are ice people and blacks are the warm kind, a race of jalapenos, which explains—well, I'm not quite sure what it explains, though it sure makes some blacks feel awfully warm inside. Ethnic cheerleading on the lunatic fringe gets raunchy; this fellow tells his audience that Jews, in particular, are as icy as they get. And anyhow, he won't let white students into his courses at CUNY!

Well, kooks are kooks, and it's healthy for a normal and powerful group to have its kooks. Why should they be better than anybody else? White Protestants have their Duke, so blacks can have their Jeffries. But while it is common knowledge that, in the quite reputable and important academic field of Afro-American studies, this fellow is a disgrace and an embarrassment, you don't often hear the scholars of that field saying so. They don't want to break ranks. So some get the impression that "blacks are a bunch of self-segregated haters and racists," which isn't fair or true, even though the good folks who bring us the likes of Professor Jeffries to celebrate "black awareness" up at USF want us to think that he speaks for all and to all blacks. If any African-American students at USF said otherwise, it wasn't in a very loud voice.

Then again, on my side of the bay, we have the impression that all blacks want to get rid of Curtsinger and all whites want to keep him, since rare are the voices on the white side that speak against him, and no black leader thinks the firing was wrong. No one, on either side, broke ranks: no black tells us Curtsinger was treated shabbily and denied due process, though he was; no white tells us Curtsinger failed to win the confidence of a powerful component of St. Petersburg's social order, though he manifestly failed even the simplest tests of common sense in race relations.

The list gets longer when you leave Tampa Bay. For many years, the great Catholic theologian and sociologist, Andrew Greeley, warned the Catholic Church about the problem of pedophilia in the Catholic priesthood. He was dismissed as a renegade. Now, his cardinal in Chicago has recognized the problem was there all the time—and is solving it. Father Greeley "broke ranks." But he told the truth when it had to be told, and enormous suffering and humiliation of the priesthood would have been prevented had people paid attention.

All these examples point to a single fact. Some members of minorities (and most of us are minorities in some way, even Bubba with his pick up truck and six pack, I suppose) want to segregate themselves: Fight in private, put up a united front in public. Not uncommonly, the self-segregationists also are the ones who want to control what the united front stands for. So the argument for a united front turns out to plea for "our crowd" to run things just the way it wants.

But we're all free to speak our minds in public (there is no other freedom worth having, self-censorship being the alternative). It's a statement of confidence in a free society to speak your mind in public—and a statement of decent respect for the wit and good will of fellow citizens, who are rarely fooled, or even impressed, by united fronts.

Well then, is it all right to argue in public? I say, it had better be, because in this free and open society of ours, try to keep a secret!

Chapter 23

A Concluding Affirmation: Jews, Judaism, and Abortion

Lehayyim—"To Life"

So many Jewish institutions, religious and eleemosynary, and individuals speaking (as they say) "as Jews" favor unrestricted abortion that pro-life circles suppose Judaism, as distinct from individual Jews, does too. But as soon as we distinguish the personal opinion of individuals from the doctrines of a faith set forth in authoritative holy books, matters prove more complex. Not only so, but when we realize that from the time of Spinoza to the present, not all those who identified themselves as Jews professed the religion, Judaism, so that some Jews also are Judaists and some not, we recognize a considerable error. It is to confuse public opinion among Jews, which tends in the aggregate to favor liberal over conservative positions in politics, with the theological judgment of Judaism as set forth in the Torah.

Ample cause for doubt that the religion, Judaism, without restriction of any kind, favors abortion and treats the fetus as null, derives from Orthodox Judaism, which in all of its rich variety has uniformly objected to the prevailing characterization of the Judaic (as distinct from the Jewish-ethnic) position on the question. But only just now has a broadly circulated essay, "a Torah-view of abortion," by the distinguished Orthodox Judaic religious leader, Rabbi Shlomo Riskin, an American who has settled in the state of Israel in Efrat, provided a clear and succinct account of the matter. Riskin quite perspicaciously saw the issue of abortion on demand in Exodus 21:22-23: "and if two men strive together and hurt a woman, causing her to miscarry, and there is no fatal harm, he shall surely be fined . . . But if fatal injury follows, then you shall give life for life." Riskin quite properly reads the "fatal injury" to refer to the woman, not the unborn child, and he calls attention to the well established law of the Mishnah (the authoritative second century law code on which the Talmud of Babylonia is constructed), that "one life cannot set aside another life." In consequence, if a woman is in danger of life, even in labor, the unborn child is to be destroyed so as to save the life of the mother. The rule of course is monumentally irrelevant to the contemporary debate, since it is not the life but the convenience of the mother that is, in general, at stake; to put matters more charitably, it is never that abortion limited to the purpose of saving the woman's life that abortionists advocate.

But that ruling has slight, if any, relevance to the stakes in the debate on abortion on demand. The real question is other: is the fetus considered a life that is sacred? The answer is unequivocally that it is. The Babylonian Talmud takes the position that if a pregnant woman dies on the Sabbath, if it is possible to remove the fetus so that the child may survive, one is to violate the laws that protect the sanctity of the Sabbath in order to save the life of the fetus. That ruling provides unambiguous evidence on the issue at hand. Since the law maintains that the Sabbath's sanctity may be violated only to save a human life, the ruling clearly rests upon the premise that the unborn child is a fully human life. The Babylonian Talmud further holds that life begins when the soul and body are united, which is the fortieth day beyond conception.

Riskin asks, "Can we call a fetus a full-fledged life, with complete rights and full protection entitled for all human beings?" He finds his answer in the legal code of Moses Maimonides (1194-1270), who is a principal authority for Judaism. The reason that the law-code is theologically indicative is simple. Judaism frames its theological opinions through rulings on what people may or may not do, in the theory that what we do makes an authoritative statement on what we are—and what we aim to be—in God's image, after God's likeness. Accordingly, if we want to find the authoritative theological ruling on any given question, we start with the normative account of how people are supposed to behave. From that concrete and irreducible fact we proceed to extrapolate the theological principle that is thereby expressed. In the issue at hand, to grasp Maimonides' view—which enjoys the authority and standing of the view of Judaism, absent later, contrary, and widely accepted ruling, of which, in this case, there is none—we shall have to move in two distinct steps.

The first is his explanation of why, if the fetus is inside the womb, the mother's life takes precedence; when the head has emerged, that is not the fact, because one life is not set aside in favor of another. Maimonides' reason for this ruling on the face of it is somewhat jarring. He says, "we are obligated to destroy the fetus because the fetus is considered a pursuer, in effect, a murderer," in threatening the life of the mother. Riskin notes that, in his laws of murder, Maimonides rules that "if we come upon a potential murderer clutching a knife in hot pursuit of someone in flight, we are obligated to do what it takes to stop the pursuer, even if it means killing him" (a ruling that the New York courts would do well to contemplate!). Riskin then comments, "By placing the law of abortion within the framework of the laws of murder, and then, offering the analogy of the fetus to the legal position of a potential murder, who is to be destroyed, Maimonides opens the nature of the fetus for detailed analysis." In point of fact, to state matters negatively, Maimonides does not classify the fetus as a mere limb or an organ of the mother's body. The analogy that he invokes treats the fetus as a being in its own right. It is not part of the mother. It is a potential life, and, Riskin says, "One cannot get rid of the fetus at will."

The fetus may be part of the mother, Judaism maintains in Riskin's reading, but that does not mean the mother owns the fetus or is free to dispose of him or her at whim. He says, "Treating a human life seriously means that we have to treat potential human life seriously as well. If the mother cannot destroy her own life, she cannot destroy a life that is not hers, either." If the fetus threatens the life of the mother, it must be destroyed, and the law of Judaism recognizes as life-threatening physical and also psychological dangers, "each case to be judged on its own merits by medical and rabbinical counseling." But Riskin is explicit, and I give his judgment, well-founded as it is on the authoritative sources of Judaism: "When no mitigating circumstances exist, and the proposed abortion proves to be only a desire to get rid of an inconvenience, Jewish law . . . clearly forbids the taking of potential life."

That is, pure and simple, the view of Judaism on abortion at whim, on fetus-cide, on "pro-choice," and on a variety of other issues that affect the sanctity of life. Judaism is a life-affirming religious tradition, seeing humanity "in God's image, after God's likeness," and maintaining that the human being is "in God's image," not only after emerging from the womb, but from the fortieth day onward within the womb. That is not a position that is identical to the Roman Catholic and Christian orthodox one, but it is entirely congruent and only marginally asymmetrical. Accordingly, when we hear that "Judaism" affirms the "right" of women to abort their babies, the correct theological response is simple: (some, perhaps many) Jews may take that position, but the authoritative voice of Judaism, which is the Torah, as mediated by the great sages through time, recognizes no such right, because the Torah affirms life and, specifically and explicitly, the right to life also of the fetus in the womb.

Like abolition of chattel-slavery in the mid-nineteenth century, so the affirmation of life in the end of the twentieth century forms the critical issue of the social order. That seems to me appropriate, because this has been a century of death on a cosmopolitan scale. We Jews, of course, have suffered disproportionately (or so it seems to us; the Cambodians have good reason to demur, so too the Armenians). With a million dead on the Marne and two million before Verdun, with ten million starved to death in the Ukraine, twenty million Soviet citizens in World War II, not to mention the millions of Chinese wantonly killed by the Japanese in World War II, and the tens of thousands of Japanese who died in atomic explosions and the millions more who died in battle, and the list goes on and on—with all that killing, one mass murder, more or less, will scarcely make the case more persuasive. The affirmation of life in the face of death in this bloody century should define the critical existential task.

The issue of abortion faced me personally, and in a deeply Jewish context; it is not a matter of mere theological and legal theory. On the eve of the New Year, in September 1973, my father-in-law died in a swimming accident in Jerusalem. My wife and I flew over to bury him where he wanted, in the holy city of Judaism. His death could have happened this morning, so far as I am concerned; I was never reconciled to it. We came home just in time to hear the early reports of the Yom Kippur War, in which our private mourning joined with the public mourning for thousands of young Israelis, killed in the crisis of an army unprepared for battle. Within days of the end of the fighting, we discovered that, because of a faulty IUD, we were expecting a new baby. With four children to raise, a fifth unanticipated at a very painful and wrenching time, came to us as an extraordinary blessing. It never entered our mind not to rejoice, not for one instant; it seemed to us some sort of small remedy for all the death round about.

The doctor warned that the baby might be damaged by the IUD and that the baby might not survive to term. So there was a clear choice of whether or not to abort. We decided, without a moment of hesitation, "to life," and no more death. If the baby were born, we would find it a consolation and a joy; we would take our chances. We did. The IUD, which had permitted the pregnancy, aborted it; at the fifth month, under trying circumstances, we had a miscarriage, and I found myself delivering the fetus. It was then, in February 1974, that, in the deep layers of my being, following instinct more than reason, I recognize the fundamental truth that the sanctity of life—which in Judaism extends to the preparation of the food we eat—begins in the womb, not afterward. Only later on did I pursue the question of the authoritative position of Judaism so ably expounded now, in an authoritative way, by Rabbi Riskin.

Every time we Jews take a drink of wine, we say, "To life." I am confident that with a deepening reflection on the meaning of that phrase, more and more Jews will recognize, in this context, what that "to life" means. It is, as Rabbi Riskin says: "When no mitigating circumstances exist, and the proposed abortion proves to be only a desire to get rid of an inconvenience, Jewish law . . . clearly forbids the taking of potential life."

More Good Books From Huntington House Publishers

Recent Releases

Gays & Guns
The Case Against Homosexuals in the Military
by John Eidsmoe

The homosexual revolution seeks to overthrow the Laws of Nature. A Lieutenant Colonel in the United States Air Force Reserve, Dr. John Eidsmoe eloquently contends that admitting gays into the military would weaken the combat effectiveness of our armed forces. This cataclysmic step would also legitimize homosexuality, a lifestyle that most Americans know is wrong.

While echoing Cicero's assertion that "a sense of what is right is common to all mankind," Eidsmoe rationally defends his belief. There are laws that govern the universe, he reminds us. Laws that compel the earth to rotate on its axis, laws that govern the economy; and so there is also a moral law that governs man's nature. The violation of this moral law is physically, emotionally and spiritually destructive. It is destructive to both the individual and to the community of which he is a member.

ISBN Trade Paper 1-56384-043-X $7.99
ISBN Hardcover 1-56384-046-4 $14.99

Trojan Horse—
How the New Age Movement Infiltrates the Church
by Samantha Smith & Brenda Scott

New Age/Occult concepts and techniques are being introduced into all major denominations. The revolution is subtle, cumulative, and deadly. Through what door has this heresy entered the church? Authors Samantha Smith and Brenda Scott attempt to demonstrate that Madeleine L'Engle has been and continues to be a major New Age source of entry into the church. Because of her radical departure from traditional Christian theology, Madeleine L'Engle's writings have sparked a wave of controversy across the nation. She has been published and promoted by numerous magazines, including *Today's Christian Woman, Christianity Today* and others. The deception, unfortunately, has been so successful that otherwise discerning congregations and pastors have fallen into the snare that has been laid.

Sadly, many Christians are embracing the demonic doctrines of the New Age movement. Well hidden under "Christian" labels, occult practices, such as Zen meditation, altered states, divinations, out of body experences, "discovering the Divine truth within" and others have defiled many. This book explores the depths of infiltration and discusses ways to combat it.

ISBN 1-56384-040-5 $9.99

A Jewish Conservative Looks at Pagan America
by Don Feder

With eloquence and insight that rival contemporary commentators and essayists of antiquity, Don Feder's pen finds his targets in the enemies of God, family, and American tradition and morality. Deftly ... delightfully ... the master allegorist and Titian with a typewriter brings clarity to the most complex sociological issues and invokes giggles and wry smiles from both followers and foes. Feder is Jewish to the core, and he finds in his Judaism no inconsistency with an American Judeo-Christian ethic. Questions of morality plague school administrators, district court judges, senators, congressmen, parents, and employers; they are wrestling for answers in a "changing world." Feder challenges this generation and directs inquirers to the original books of wisdom: the Torah and the Bible.

ISBN 1-56384-036-7 Trade Paper $9.99
ISBN 1-56384-037-5 Hardcover $19.99

Don't Touch That Dial:
The Impact of the Media on Children and the Family
by Barbara Hattemer & Robert Showers

Men and women without any stake in the outcome of the war between the pornographers and our families have come to the qualified, professional agreement that media does have an effect on our children—an effect that is devastatingly significant. Highly respected researchers, psychologists, and sociologists join a bevy of pediatricians, district attorneys, parents, teachers, pastors, and community leaders—who have diligently remained true to the fight against pornographic media—in their latest comprehensive critique of the modern media establishment (i.e., film, television, print, art, curriculum).

ISBN 1-56384-032-4 Trade Paper $9.99
ISBN 1-56384-035-9 Hardcover $19.99

Political Correctness:
The Cloning of the American Mind
by David Thibodaux, Ph.D.

The author, a professor of literature at the University of Southwestern Louisiana, confronts head on the movement that is now being called Political Correctness. Political correctness, says Thibodaux, "is an umbrella under which advocates of civil rights, gay and lesbian rights, feminism, and environmental causes have gathered." To incur the wrath of these groups, one only has to disagree with them on political, moral, or social issues. To express traditionally Western concepts in universities today can result in not only ostracism, but even suspension. (According to a recent "McNeil-Lehrer News Hour" report, one student was suspended for discussing the reality of the moral law with an avowed homosexual. He was reinstated only after he apologized.)

ISBN 1-56384-026-X Trade Paper $9.99

Subtle Serpent:
New Age in the Classroom
by Darylann Whitemarsh & Bill Reisman

There is a new morality being taught to our children in public schools. Without the consent or even awareness of parents—educators and social engineers are aggressively introducing new moral codes to our children. In most instances, these new moral codes contradict traditional values. Darylann Whitemarsh (a 1989 Teacher of the Year recipient) and Bill Reisman (educator and expert on the occult) combine their knowledge to expose the deliberate madness occurring in our public schools.

ISBN 1-56384-016-2 $9.99

When the Wicked Seize a City
by Chuck & Donna McIlhenny with Frank York

A highly publicized lawsuit... a house fire-bombed in the night... the shatter of windows smashed by politically (and wickedly) motivated vandals cuts into the night.... All this because Chuck McIlhenny voiced God's condemnation of a behavior and life-style and protested the destruction of society that results from its practice. That behavior is homosexuality, and that life-style is the gay culture. This book explores: the rise of gay power and what it will mean if Christians do not organize and prepare for the battle.

ISBN 1-56384-024-3 $9.99

Loyal Opposition:
A Christian Response to the Clinton Agenda
by John Edismoe

The night before the November 1992 elections, a well-known evangelist claims to have had a dream. In this dream, he says, God told him that Bill Clinton would be elected President, and Christians should support his Presidency. **What are we to make of this?** Does it follow that, because God **allowed** Clinton to be President; therefore, God **wants** Clinton to be president? Does God **want** everything that God **allows**? Is it possible for an event to occur even though that event displeases God? **How do we stand firm in our opposition to the administration's proposals when those proposals contradict Biblical values?** And how do we organize and work effectively for constructive action to restore our nation to basic values?

ISBN 1-56384-044-8 $7.99

BACKLIST/BEST-SELLERS

Deadly Decepti[on]
by Jim Shaw & Tom McKen[ney]

For the first time the 33 degree ritual is made public! Learn of [the] "secrets" and "deceptions" that are practiced daily around the wo[rld]. Find out why Freemasonry teaches that it is the true religion, that [all] other religions are only corrupted and perverted forms of Free[ma]sonry. If you know anyone in the Masonic movement, you must r[ead] this book.

ISBN 0-910311-54-4 $7

Exposing the AI[DS] Scan[dal]
by Dr. Paul Came[ron]

Where do you turn when those who control the flow of informat[ion] in this country withhold the truth? Why is the national media hid[ing] facts from the public? Can AIDS be spread in ways we're not being t[old]? Finally, a book that gives you a total account for the AIDS epider[mic] and what steps can be taken to protect yourself. What you don't k[now] can kill you!

ISBN 0-910311-52-8 $7

Hidden Dangers of t[he] Rainb[ow]
by Constance Cum[bey]

The first book to uncover and expose the New Age movement, t[his] national #1 best-seller paved the way for all other books on the subj[ect]. It has become a giant in its category. This book provides the v[ital] expose of the New Age movement, which the author contend[s is] dedicated to wiping out Christianity and establishing a one w[orld] order. This movement, a vast network of occult and pagan organ[iza]tions, meets the tests of prophecy concerning the Antichrist.

ISBN 0-910311-03-X $8

Kinsey, Sex and Fraud: The Indoctrination of a People
by Dr. Judith A. Reisman and Edward Eichel

Kinsey, Sex and Fraud describes the research of Alfred Kinsey which shaped Western society's beliefs and understanding of the nature of human sexuality. His unchallenged conclusions are taught at every level of education—elementary, high school and college—and quoted in textbooks as undisputed truth.

The authors clearly demonstrate that Kinsey's research involved illegal experimentations on several hundred children. The survey was carried out on a non-representative group of Americans, including disproportionately large numbers of sex offenders, prostitutes, prison inmates and exhibitionists.

ISBN 0-910311-20-X Hardcover $19.99

Journey into Darkness: Nowhere to Land
by Stephen L. Arrington

This story begins on Hawaii's glistening sands and ends in the mysterious deep of the Great White Shark. In between, he found himself trapped in the drug smuggling trade—unwittingly becoming the "Fall Guy" in the highly publicized John Z. DeLorean drug case. Naval career shattered, his youthful innocence tested, and friends and family put to the test of loyalty, Arrington locked on one truth during his savage stay in prison and endeavors to share that critical truth now. Focusing on a single important message to young people—to stay away from drugs—the author recounts his horrifying prison experience and allows the reader to take a peek at the source of hope and courage that helped him survive.

ISBN 1-56384-003-3 $9.99

"Soft Porn" Plays Hardball
by Dr. Judith A. Reisman

With amazing clarity, the author demonstrates that pornography imposes on society a view of women and children that encourages violence and sexual abuse. As crimes against women and children increase to alarming proportions, it's of paramount importance that we recognize the cause of this violence. Pornography should be held accountable for the havoc it has wreaked in our homes and our country.

ISBN 0-910311-65-X Trade Paper $8.99
ISBN 0-910311-92-7 Hardcover $16.95

ORDER THESE HUNTINGTON HOUSE BOOKS!

	Title	Price	
____	America Betrayed—Marlin Maddoux	$6.99	____
____	Angel Vision (A Novel)—Jim Carroll with Jay Gaines	5.99	____
____	Battle Plan: Equipping the Church for the 90s—Chris Stanton	7.99	____
____	Blessings of Liberty—Charles C. Heath	8.99	____
____	Crystalline Connection (A Novel)—Bob Maddux	8.99	____
____	Deadly Deception: Freemasonry—Tom McKenney	7.99	____
____	The Delicate Balance—John Zajac	8.99	____
____	Dinosaurs and the Bible—Dave Unfred	12.99	____
____	*Don't Touch That Dial—Barbara Hattemer & Robert Showers	9.99/19.99	____
____	En Route to Global Occupation—Gary Kah	9.99	____
____	Exposing the AIDS Scandal—Dr. Paul Cameron	7.99	____
____	Face the Wind—Gloria Delaney	9.99	____
____	*False Security—Jerry Parks	9.99	____
____	From Rock to Rock—Eric Barger	8.99	____
____	*Gays & Guns—John Eidsmoe	7.99	____
____	Hidden Dangers of the Rainbow—Constance Cumbey	8.99	____
____	*Hitler and the New Age—Bob Rosio	9.99	____
____	Inside the New Age Nightmare—Randall Baer	8.99	____
____	*A Jewish Conservative Looks at Pagan America—Don Feder	9.99/19.99	____
____	*Journey Into Darkness—Stephen Arrington	9.99	____
____	Kinsey, Sex and Fraud—Dr. Judith A. Reisman & Edward Eichel (Hard cover)	19.99	____
____	Last Days Collection—Last Days Ministries	8.95	____
____	Legend of the Holy Lance (A Novel)—William T. Still	8.99/16.99	____
____	New World Order—William T. Still	8.99	____
____	*One Year to a College Degree—Lynette Long & Eileen Hershberger	9.99	____
____	*Political Correctness—David Thibodaux	9.99	____
____	Psychic Phenomena Unveiled—John Anderson	8.99	____
____	* Real Men—Dr. Harold Voth	9.99	____
____	"Soft Porn" Plays Hardball—Dr. Judith A. Reisman	8.99/16.95	____
____	*Subtle Serpent—Darylann Whitemarsh & Bill Reisman	9.99	____
____	Teens and Devil-Worship—Charles G.B. Evans	8.99	____
____	To Grow By Storybook Readers—Janet Friend	44.95 per set	____
____	Touching the Face of God—Bob Russell (Paper/Hardcover)	8.99/18.99	____
____	Trojan Horse—Brenda Scott & Samantha Smith	9.99	____
____	Twisted Cross—Joseph Carr	9.99	____
____	*When the Wicked Seize a City—Chuck & Donna McIlhenny with Frank York	9.99	____
____	Who Will Rule the Future?—Paul McGuire	8.99	____
____	*You Hit Like a Girl—Elsa Houtz & William J. Ferkile	9.99	____
	Shipping and Handling		____
*New Title	**Total**		____

AVAILABLE AT BOOKSTORES EVERYWHERE or order direct from:
Huntington House Publishers • P.O. Box 53788 • Lafayette, LA 70505
Send check/money order. For faster service use VISA/MASTERCARD
call toll-free 1-800-749-4009.

Add: Freight and handling, $3.50 for the first book ordered, and $.50 for each additional book up to 5 books.

Enclosed is $_____ including postage.
VISA/MASTERCARD#_____ Exp. Date_____
Name_____ Phone: (   )_____
Address_____
City, State, Zip_____